INTRODUCTION.

The publications which I have presented to the world, having been almost exclusively confined to subjects connected with the Fine Arts, I feel it in some measure incumbent on me to explain the cause of my having undertaken to be the publisher of this volume. It has arisen from a distressing event, in which its very ingenious, useful, and elaborate Author, happened to be involved. The work was in some degree of advancement, when the sudden and most unexpected misfortune to which I have alluded, threw him at once into a state of discouragement, that gave a check to all his exertions. I, who had known him long, and had every reason, from a most intimate acquaintance, to think well of him, both in his private as well as professional character, co-operated with many of his friends, some of whom are in the superior ranks of life, to encourage him in the renewal of his former energy—but I could succeed no further than in prevailing upon him to complete this little work on Culinary Philosophy, which promised to be highly useful in some of the leading objects of Domestic Economy. When it was ready for publication, the prejudice which had been excited against him, rendered his former publishers averse from presenting it to the public. I therefore felt myself under a kind of indispensable engagement— nor am I ashamed of it, as the work was brought to a state of publication by my interference, though out of my usual line of business, to become its publisher. I accordingly, under these circumstances, made it my own by purchasing the copy-right. Nor, from its scientific novelty, and promised utility, have I the least hesitation in presenting Mr. Accum's Work to the Public.

R. ACKERMANN.

PREFACE.

LONDON,
COMPTON STREET, SOHO.

The following pages are intended to exhibit a popular view of the philosophy of cookery, to enable the reader to understand the chemical principles, by means of which alimentary substances are rendered palatable and nutritious. The subject may appear frivolous; but let it be remembered that it is by the application of the principles of philosophy to the ordinary affairs of life, that science diffuses her benefits, and perfects her claim to the gratitude of mankind.

The art of preparing good and wholesome food is, undoubtedly, a branch of chemistry; the kitchen is a chemical laboratory; all the processes employed for rendering alimentary substances fit for human sustenance, are chemical processes; and much waste of the materials, as well as labour to the parties, might often be spared, were those who practise this art, made acquainted with some simple chemical truths which invariably would lead to certain results.

I have, in the first place, premised, as introductory to what follows, some general observations on the various kinds of alimentary substances commonly used for food; in which I have noticed their chemical constitution, and comparative nutritive qualities.

After these preliminary statements, I have proceeded to explain the summary processes of the culinary art, as practised in the English kitchen, to render obvious the chemical effects produced by the operations of roasting, boiling, stewing, broiling, frying, and other means employed for dressing food.

I have given concise, but accurate directions for preparing good and wholesome pickles, and other condiments employed in domestic economy.

I have pointed out the rules to be attended to in the art of conserving recent fruits, and other vegetable substances, in the state of what are called preserves, marmalades, fruit jams, and jellies, to enable the reader to prepare those kinds of comfitures with economy and success.

I have given concise directions for preserving butcher's meat, fish, and fowl, after being cooked, to render them fit for sea store, or domestic use, at a future time.

I have stated the most approved processes for curing bacon, hams, smoked beef, and salted fish; to which I have added instructions for the choice of butcher's meat, and the best methods of constructing pantries, larders, and meat safes.

I have pointed out the loss of weight which different kinds of meat suffers in the usual operations of cooking.

I have described the most approved methods for preserving recently gathered fruits in their natural state, as nearly as possible, with directions for constructing fruit rooms, and the circumstances to be attended to in storing esculent roots and other vegetables.

I have animadverted on certain material errors, sometimes committed through ignorance or negligence, in the preparation of food, and various delicacies of the table; and I have also given hints that will be found useful, with regard to the practice of making tea and coffee. And lastly, I have made some remarks on the construction of kitchen fire-places, to which I have added designs, exhibiting the most approved cooking apparatus, calculated for the use of private families or public establishments.

In resuming the whole, I have endeavoured (and I hope with some degree of success,) to communicate to those to whom the superintendance of a family is entrusted, such useful culinary information as may lead to beneficial consequences.

Cookery.

COOKERY IS A BRANCH OF CHEMICAL SCIENCE.

Cookery, or the art of preparing good and wholesome food, and of preserving all sorts of alimentary substances in a state fit for human sustenance, of rendering that agreeable to the taste which is essential to the support of life, and of pleasing the palate without injury to the system, is, strictly speaking, a branch of chemistry; but, important as it is both to our enjoyments and our health, it is also one of the least cultivated branches of that science. The culinary processes of roasting, boiling, baking, stewing, frying, broiling, the art of preserving meats, bacon, and hams; the preparations of sauces, pickles, and other condiments; the conserving of fruits; the care and keeping of vegetables; the making of jellies, jams, and marmalades, are all founded upon the principles of this science, and much waste of the material, as well as labour to the parties might often be spared, were those to whom the performance of such tasks is committed, made acquainted with simple chemical truths which would invariably lead to certain results. And, besides, the same knowledge would enable them to attain a much greater degree of perfection in curing and preserving all kinds of animal and vegetable aliments, and in combining the three grand requisites of taste, nutriment, and salubrity, in whatever manner they may be prepared. And, though this art is at present in rude hands, as all branches of chemistry were originally, there is no reason that it should remain so. A kitchen is, in fact, a chemical laboratory; the boilers, stew-pans, and cradle spit of the cook, correspond to the digestors, the evaporating basins, and the crucibles of the chemist. And numerous as the receipts of cookery are, the general operations (like the general process of chemistry) are but few. In some the object aimed at is, to extract the constituent parts of the food, so as to exhibit them in a separate state, or to combine them with other substances, to produce new compounds which differ widely from those from which they originated. In others, the qualities of the substances are simply altered by the action of fire, to render them more palatable and nutritious.

From the multiplicity of circumstances to be attended to in this art, the whole of which is founded upon the principles of chemistry, we may easily see that it must be a very precarious one; and, there is reason to believe, that among the variety of circumstances which produce diseases, the improper modes of cooking food, are often the primary cause. Will it be believed, that in the cookery books which form the prevailing oracles of the kitchens in this part of the island, there are express injunctions to *"boil greens with halfpence, or verdigrise,* in order to improve their *colour!"*[1] That our puddings are frequently seasoned with laurel leaves, and our sweatmeats almost uniformly prepared in copper vessels?[2] Why are we thus compelled to swallow a supererogatory quantity of poison which may so easily be avoided? And why are we constantly made to run the risk of our lives by participating in custards, trifles, and blancmanges, seasoned by a most deadly poison extracted from the *prunus lourocerasus*?[3] Verily, where such detestable systems of cookery are practised, we may exclaim with the sacred historian, that there is "Death in the Pot."

[1] The Ladies Library, vol. ii. p. 203; and also Modern Cookery, 2nd Edition, p. 94.

[2] Literary Chronicle, No. xxii. p. 348, 1819.

[3] Philosophical Magazine, No. cclviii. vol. 54, p. 317.

Food badly cooked is wasted to no purpose. It seems to have been a complaint familiar in the mouth of our ancestors, and which we have too often seen reason to re-echo in the present day—*"That God sends good meat, but the devil sends cooks."*

OBSERVATIONS ON THE FOOD OF MAN.

No animal eats such variety of food as man; he claims, more justly than any other creature, the title of *omnivorous!* for since he is distinguished beyond all animals, but the capability of living in the most distant parts of the globe, under every variety of climate which the earth affords, his food could not be confined exclusively to either the vegetable or animal kingdom, because he inhabits regions that afford aliments widely different from each other. Cattle content themselves with green vegetables; rapacious animals live on the flesh of other creatures.

Those of the Linnæan order, *glires*,[4] live on grain and fruits; each order of birds, keeps, in the same manner, to one sort of food, animal or vegetable. Fishes, reptiles, and insects, also have each their peculiar and exclusive bill of fare, beyond which even hunger will scarcely force them to wander. But however various each class, and order, and species of animated nature may be in the choice of food, man—all-devouring man, will embrace the whole range of the creation, "scarce a berry or a mushroom can escape him."

[4] The hare, rabbit, guinea-pig, &c.

With the lion and the wolf he will eat of fresh slain animals; with the dogs and the vulture he will feed on putrid flesh;[5] with the ox and the guinea-pig he will devour raw vegetables, under the name of salads; with the squirrel and the mouse he will feast on nuts and grain; with birds of prey he feeds on fowl of almost every species; with fishes he feeds on fish; and with insects and reptiles he sometimes lives on insects and reptiles. Nor is he satisfied even with this abundant variety, but must go to the mineral kingdom for salt, as a condiment before he can furnish out his meal.

[5] Every person knows in what a putrid state game is often eaten.

NATIONS LIVING WHOLLY UPON VEGETABLE FOOD.

The variety of alimentary substances used not only by individuals, but among whole nations, are prodigiously diversified, and climate seems to have some effect in producing the diversity of taste, though it must in a great measure depend upon the natural productions of particular countries, their religion, and their commercial intercourse.

A vegetable diet seems suitable to the hot countries under the Equator, and we accordingly find nations there, who have completely adopted it, and who abstain so much the more from all animal food, in as much as it is an article of their religious faith.

Potatoes, chesnuts, and the leguminous and cereal seeds, satisfy the want of the Alpine peasant, and numerous tribes solely feed on vegetables and water. In the most remote antiquity, we read of whole nations in Africa, and of the Indian priests, who lived entirely on vegetable substances. Some wandering Moors subsist almost entirely on gum senegal.

NATIONS LIVING WHOLLY ON ANIMAL FOOD.

The nations which live on animal food are very numerous.

The Ethiopeans, Scythians, and Arabians, ate nothing but flesh.

The miserable inhabitants of New Holland lived wholly on fish when that country was first discovered, and other tribes on the Arabian and Persian gulph.

In the Faro islands, in Iceland and Greenland, the food arises from the same source.

The shepherds in the province of Caracas, on the Oronoko, live wholly on flesh. The Tartars in Asia, and some savage nations in North America, live on raw and half putrid flesh, and some barbarous tribes eat their meat raw.

It appears to be the effect of climate and religion that makes the Hindoo adopt vegetable rather than animal food; it is the effect of natural production that makes the Greenlander relish whale-blubber and train-oil. It is to one or other of these causes that we must refer all such diversity of national tastes, though it would be difficult in many cases to separate the influence of each. We see the Englishman enjoying his under-done roast beef and his plum-pudding; the Scotsman his hodge-podge and his haggis; the Frenchman his ragouts, omlets, and fricandeaus; the German his sour-crout, sausages, and smoked hams, the Italian his maccaroni; and the Tartar his horse-flesh.[6] *"De gustibus non est disputandum."*—There is no disputing about tastes. They are too many, and too various, to be objects of rational discussion.

[6] An article of food which has lately been seriously recommended by Mr. Grey to Europeans as a most advantageous measure of political economy.

SINGULAR KIND OF ALIMENTS OF VARIOUS NATIONS.

Besides the before-mentioned diversities of national and individual taste for different kinds of substances, used as aliments, there are other kinds of food which we at least think more singular. Some of the tribes of Arabs, Moors, the Californians, and Ethiopians, eat tad-poles, locusts, and spiders.

In some places the flesh of serpents, that of the *coluber natrix* for example, is eaten; and the viper is made into broth. Several other reptiles are used as food by the European settlers in America, such as the *rana bombina* and *rana taurina*, two species of toads.

In the East, the *lacerta scincus* is considered a great luxury, and also an approdisiac. Even the rattle snake has been eaten, and the head boiled along with the rest of the body of the animal.

The horse, ass, and camel, are eaten in several regions of the earth, and the seal, walruss, and Arctic bear, have often yielded a supply to sailors.

On the singular taste of epicures it is not necessary to speak. Mæcenas, the prime minister of Augustus, and refined patron of Horace, had young asses served upon his table when he treated his friends; and, according to Pliny,[7] the Romans delighted in the flavour of young and well fattened puppies. This strange practice subsists still in China, and among the Esquimaux. Plump, and well roasted bats, laid upon a bed of olives, are eaten in the Levant as a dainty.

[7] 2 Book 29, c. 4.

The Roman luxury, *garum*, which bore so high a price, consisted of the putrid entrails of fishes, (first of the *garum*,) stewed in wine, and a similar dish is still considered as a great luxury, in some parts of the East. Some modern epicures delight in the trail of the woodcock, and even collect with care the contents of the intestines which distill from it in the process of roasting.

> "*The Irishman* loves usquebah,
>   *The Scot* loves ale called blue cap,
> *The Welshman*, he loves toasted cheese,
>   And makes his mouth like a mouse trap."

Apicius,[8] among other whimsical personages of ancient Rome, presented to his guests ragouts, exclusively composed of tongues of peacocks and nightingales. This celebrated epicure, who instituted a gormandizing academy at Rome, having heard that shrimps and prawns of a superior flavour were to be met with on the coasts of Africa than on the Italian shore, freighted a ship, and sailed in search of these far famed marine insects. This person spent more than £.60,000 merely to vary the taste of culinary sauces.

> [8] Three brothers of that name were celebrated at Rome, on account of their unparallelled love of good eating.

Vitellus was treated by his brother with a dinner, consisting of 2,000 dishes of fish, and 7,000 of poultry—surely this is not doing things by halves.

A Mr. Verditch de Bourbonne[9] is said to have bought 3,000 carps for the mere sake of their tongues, which were brought, well seasoned and *learnedly* dressed, to his table, in one dish.

> [9] Cours Gastronomique.

DIFFERENCE BETWEEN AN EPICURE AND A GLUTTON.

However extravagant and whimsical the rational pleasures of the table may appear to a *sober* and sensible mind, we must, in justice to epicures, cursorily observe, that there exists a material difference between a *gormand* or epicure, and a *glutton*.[10] The first seeks for peculiar delicacy and distinct flavour in the various dishes presented to the judgment and enjoyment of his discerning palate; while the other lays aside nearly all that relates to the rational pleasures of creating or stimulating an appetite of the cates, and looks merely to quantity; this, has his stomach in view, and tries how heavy it may be laden, without endangering his health.

> [10] *Tabella Cibaria*, a latin poem, relating to the pleasures of Gastronomy, and the mysterious art of Cooking, page 15.

"The *gormand* never loses sight of the exquisite organs of taste, so admirably disposed by Providence in the crimson chamber, where sits the discriminating judge, the human tongue.

"The *glutton* is anathematised in the Scripture with those brutes *quorum deus venter est*. The other appears guilty of no other sin than of too great, and too minute, an attention to refinement in commercial sensuality."

Our neighbours on the other side of the channel, so famous for indulging in the worship of Comus, consider the epicure again under two distinct views, namely: as a *gormand*, or a *gourmet*. The epicure or *gormand* is defined—a man having accidentally been able to study the different tastes of eatables, does accordingly select the best food and the most pleasing to his palate. His character is that of a *practioner*. The *gourmet* speculates more than he practises, and eminently prides himself in discerning the nicest degrees, and most evanescent shades of goodness and perfection in the different subjects proposed to him. He may be designated a man, who, by sipping a few drops out of the silver cup of the vintner, can instantly tell from what country the wine comes, and its age.

The *glutton* practices without any regard to theory.

The *gormand*, or epicure, unites theory with practice.

The *gourmet* is merely theoretical.

IMPORTANCE OF THE ART OF COOKERY.

As man differs from the inferior animals in the variety of articles he feeds upon, so he differs from them no less in the preparation of these substances. Some animals, besides man, prepare their food in a particular manner. The racoon (*ursus lutor*) is said to wash his roots before he eats them; and the beaver stores his green boughs under water that their bark and young twigs may remain juicy and palatable.

The action of fire, however, has never been applied to use by any animal except man; not even monkies, with all their knacks of imitation, and all their fondness for the comforts of a fire, have ever been observed to put on a single billet of wood to keep up the fuel.

Domesticated animals, indeed, are brought to eat, and even to relish, food which has been cooked by the action of heat.

The variety of productions introduced by our different modes of preparing and preserving food is almost endless; and it appears particularly so when we compare the usages, in this respect, of various countries.

The savage of New South Wales is scarcely more knowing in the preparation of food, by means of fire, than his neighbour, the kangaroo, if the anecdote told by Turnbull be true, that one of these savages plunged his hand into boiling water to take out a fish.

Some writers have humorously designated man to be *"a cooking animal,"* and he really is so. It is one of the leading distinctions which Providence has seen meet for wise purposes to establish, when it was said that he might eat of the fruit of every tree, and the flesh of every clean beast.

When we contemplate the aliments used by men in a civilized state of existence, we soon become convinced that only a small part of our daily food can be eaten in its natural state. Many of the substances used as aliments, are disagreeable, and some even poisonous until they have been cooked. Few of them are to be had at all seasons, although produced at others in greater abundance than can be consumed.

The importance of a proper and competent knowledge of the true and rational principles of cookery, must be obvious, when it is considered that there is scarcely an individual, young or old, in any civilized country, who has not some time or other suffered severely from errors committed in the practice of this art.

"A skilful and well directed cookery abounds in chemical preparations highly salutary. There exists a salubrity of aliments suited to every age. Infancy, youth, maturity, and old age, each has its peculiar adapted food, and that not merely applicable to the powers in full vigour, but to stomachs feeble by nature, and to those debilitated by excess."[11]

[11] Ude's Cookery, p. 25.—Ibid, 23.

Without abetting the unnatural and injurious appetites of the epicure, or the blameable indulgences of the glutton, we shall not perhaps be far out in our reckoning, if we assert, that almost every person is an epicure in his own way.

There are amateurs in boiling potatoes, as particular in the details, as others in dressing beaf-stakes to the utmost nicety of a single turn. Lord Blainey, still more nice, informs us, that hams are not fit to be eaten unless boiled in Champaign. *Helluos* are not confined to salmon's bellies, but are to be found among the rudest peasants who love porridge or frumenty—

> A salmon's belly, *Helluo*, was thy fate;
> The doctor call'd, declares all help too late;
> "Mercy!" cries *Helluo*, "mercy, on my soul!
> Is there no hope?—Alas! then bring the jowl."
> *Pope's Moral Essays.*

Precision in mixing ingredients is as often and as closely laid down for the coarsest dish of the peasant as for the most guarded receipe of the Lady

Bountiful of the village. The pleasures of the table have always been highly appreciated and sedulously cultivated among civilized people of every age and nation; and, in spite of the Stoic, it must be admitted, that they are the first which we enjoy, the last we abandon, and those of which we most frequently partake.

"Cookery is the soul of every pleasure, at all times and to all ages. How many marriages have been the consequence of a meeting at dinner; how much good fortune has been the result of a good supper, at what moment of our existence are we happier than at table? there hatred and animosity are lulled to sleep, and pleasure alone reigns."

Pythagoras, in his golden verses, gives complete proof, that he was particularly nice in the choice of food, and carefully points out what will occasion indigestion and flatulency. He is precise in commanding his disciples to "*abstain from beans.*" Apicius, declares that he never knew a philosopher who refused to partake of a feast.

In later times, Dr. Johnson is well known to have been exceedingly fond of good dinners, considering them as the highest enjoyment of human life. The sentiments of our great moralist are a good answer to those who think the pleasures of the table incompatible with intellectual pursuits or mental superiority. "Some people," says the Doctor, "have a foolish way of not minding, or pretending not to mind, what they eat; for my part, I mind my belly very studiously, and very carefully, and I look upon it that he who does not mind his belly will hardly mind any thing else." Boswell, his biographer, says of him, "I never knew a man who relished good eating more than he did: and when at table, he was wholly absorbed in the business of the moment." It was one of the objects which displeased him so much in his Northern tour, that the Scots were rather ignorant of the more refined arts of cookery. A lady in the Isle of Mull, anxious to gratify him for once in a dinner, had an excellent plum-pudding prepared, at some expense, and with the utmost care; but, to her great mortification, the doctor would not taste it, because, he said, "it is totally impossible to make a plum-pudding at all fit to eat in the Isle of Mull."

Another instance of this philosopher's illiberal prejudice against Scotch cookery, may also be mentioned. A lady, at whose table the Doctor was dining, enquired how he liked their national dish, the *hotch potch*, of which he was then partaking. "*Good enough for hogs,*" said the surly philosopher. "Shall I help *you* to a little more of it?" retorted the lady. To Dr. Johnson we can add the names of two distinguished physicians, Darwin, and Beddoes, both of whom were most outrageous in their published works against the pleasures of good living; they followed however a very different practice, from what they prescribed to others, as none were more fond of good dinners than these guardians of health.

Cardinal Wolsey, we should have thought, would have had something else to mind than cooking and good eating. But no person was more anxious than he, even in the whirl of the immense public business which he had to transact, to have the most skilful cooks; for all Europe was ransacked, and no expense spared, to procure culinary operators, thoroughly acquainted with the multifarious operations of the spit, the stew-pan, and the rolling-pin.

Sir Walter Scott, has been most happy in the illustration of our ancient manners with respect to good eating, in the character of Athelstan, in the Romance of Ivanhoe.

Count Rumford has not considered the pleasure of eating, and the means that may be employed for increasing it, as unworthy the attention of a philosopher, for he says, "the enjoyments which fall to the bulk of mankind, are not so numerous as to render an attempt to increase them superfluous. And even in regard to those who have it in their power to gratify their appetites to the utmost extent of their wishes, it is surely rendering them a very important service to shew them how they may increase their pleasures without destroying their health."

In the olden time, every man of consequence had his *magister coquorum*, or *master cook*, without whom he would not think of making a day's journey; and it was often no easy matter to procure *master cooks* of talent.

By a passage of Cicero[12] we are led to understand, that among other miseries of life, which constantly attended this consular personage and eloquent orator, he laboured under the disappointment of not having an excellent cook of his own; for, he says, "*coquus meus, præter jus fervens, nihil potest imitari.*" *Except hot broth, my cook can do nothing cleverly.*

[12] *Fam.* ix. 20.

The salary of the Roman cooks was nearly £1000.[13] Mark Antony, hearing Cleopatra, whom he had invited to a splendid supper, (and who was as great a *gormand* as she was handsome,) loudly praise the elegance and delicacy of the dishes, sent for the cook, and presented him with the unexpected gift of a corporate town.—*Municipium.*

[13] Tabella Cibaria, ps. 19 and 20.

Even in our own times great skill in cookery is so highly praised by many, that a very skilful cook can often command, in this metropolis, a higher salary than a learned and pious curate.

His Majesty's first and second cooks are esquires, by their office, from a period to which, in the lawyer's phrase, the memory of man is not to the contrary. We are told by Dr. Pegge, that when Cardinal Otto, the Pope's Legate, was at Oxford, in the year 1248, his brother officiated as *magister coquinæ*, an office which has always been held as a situation of high trust and confidence.

We might defend the art of cookery on another principle, namely—on the axiom recognized in the Malthusian Political Economy, that he who causes two blades of grass to grow where only one grew before, is a benefactor to his country and to human nature. Whether or not Malthus is quite right in this, we are not competent to decide; we leave that to Say, Godwin, Ricardo, and[14] Drummond. But certainly it must in many cases be of the utmost consequence, for families in particular, when embarrassed in circumstances, to make food go twice as far as without the art and aid of rational cookery it could do. We would particularly press this remark, as it is founded on numerous facts, and places the art of cookery in a more interesting point of view than any of the other circumstances which we have been considering.

[14] Principles of Currency, and Elements of Political Economy—1820.

Cookery has often drawn down on itself the animadversions of both moralists, physicians, and wits, who have made it a subject for their vituperations and their ridicule.

So early as the time of the patriarch Isaac, the sacred historian casts blame upon Esau for being epicurean enough to transfer his birth-right for a mess of pottage.

Jacob is blamed for making savoury meat with a kid for his father, with a view to rob Esau of the paternal blessing.

Diogenes, the Cynic, meeting a young man who was going to a feast, took him up in the street and carried him home to his friends, as one who was running into evident danger had he not prevented him. The whole tribe, indeed, of the Stoics and Cynics, laughed at cookery, pretending, in their vanity and pride, to be above the desire of eating niceties. Lucian, with his inexhaustible satire, most effectually and humourously exposed these their pretences.

In our own times, we have had writers of eminence who have attacked the use of a variety of food as a dreadful evil. "Should we not think a man mad," says Addison, "who at one meal will devour fowl, flesh, and fish; swallow oil, and vinegar, salt, wines, and spices; throw down sallads of twenty different herbs, sauces of an hundred ingredients, confections, and fruits of numberless sweets and flavours? What unnatural effects must such a medley produce in the body? For my part, when I behold a table set out in all its magnificence, I fancy, that I see gouts and dropsies, fevers and lethargies, and other innumerable distempers, lying in ambuscade among the dishes."

All this, and the like is, no doubt, very plausible, and very fine, and, like many other fine speeches of modern reformers, it is more fine than just. It is indeed as good a theory as may be, that cookery is the source of most, or all, of our distempers; but withal it is *a mere theory*, and only true in a very limited degree. The truth is, that it is not cookery which is to blame, if we surfeit ourselves with its good dishes; but our own sensual and insatiable appetite, and gluttony, which prompt us to seek their gratification at the expense even of our health.

Savages, whose cookery is in the rudest state, are more apt to over-eat themselves than the veriest glutton of a luxurious and refined people; a fact, which of itself, is sufficient to prove, that it is not cookery which is the cause of gluttony and surfeiting. The savage, indeed, suffers less from his gluttony than the sedentary and refined gormand; for, after sleeping, sometimes for a whole day, after gorging himself with food, hunger again drives him forth to the chace, in which he soon gets rid of the ill-effects of his overloaded stomach. Surely cookery is not to blame for the effects of gluttony, indolence, and sedentary occupations; yet it does appear, that all its ill effects are erroneously charged to the account of the refined art of cooking.

The defence of cookery, however, which we thus bring forward to repel misrepresentation, applies only to the art of preparing good, nutritious, and wholesome food.

We cannot say one word in defence of the wretched and injurious methods but too often practised, under the name of cookery, and the highly criminal practices of adulterating food with substances deleterious to health. On this subject we have spoken elsewhere.[15]

[15] A treatise on adulterations of food, and culinary poisons, exhibiting the fraudulent sophistications of bread, beer, wine, spirituous liquors, tea, coffee, cream, confectionary, vinegar, mustard, pepper, cheese, olive oil, pickles, and other articles employed in domestic economy, and methods of detecting them.—Third edition, 1821.

"A good dinner[16] is one of the greatest enjoyments of human life; but the practice of cookery is attended with not only so many disgusting and disagreeable circumstances, and even dangers, that we ought to have some regard for those who encounter them for our pleasure."

[16] The Cook's Oracle.—Preface, p. xxxv.

DIETETICAL REMARKS ON THE CHOICE AND QUANTITY OF FOOD.

Almost every person who can afford it, eats more than is requisite for promoting the growth, and renewing the strength and waste of his body. It would be ridiculous to speak concerning the precise quantity of food necessary to support the body of different individuals. Such rules do not exist in nature. The particular state or condition of the individual, the variety of constitution, and other circumstances, must be taken into account. If, after dinner, we feel ourselves as cheerful as before, we may be assured that we have made a dietetical meal.

Much has been said of temperance. The fact is, that there is an absolute determined standard of *temperance,* the point of which must be fixed by every man's natural and unprovoked appetite, while he continues *in a state of health.* As long as a person who pursues a right habit of life, eats and drinks no more than his stomach calls for and will bear, without occasioning uneasiness of any kind to himself, he may be said to live temperate. The stomach revolts against the reverse of it; indeed, the stomach is the grand organ of the human system, it is the *conscience* of the *body,* and like that, will become uneasy if all is not right within; it speaks pretty plainly to those who lead an intemperate life.

"We may compare," says Doctor Kitchener, "the human frame to a watch, of which the heart is the main *spring,* the stomach the *regulator,* and what we put into it, the *key,* by which the machine is set a-going; according to the quantity, quality, and proper digestion of what we eat and drink will be the action of the system: and when a due proportion is preserved between the quantum of exercise and that of excitement, all goes well. If the machine be disordered, the same expedients are employed for its re-adjustment, as are used by the watch-maker; it must be carefully cleaned and then judiciously oiled. To affirm that such a thing is wholesome, or unwholesome, without considering the subject in all the circumstances to which it bears relation, and the unaccountable idiosyncrasies of particular constitutions is, with submission, talking nonsense. Every man must consult his stomach; whatever agrees with that perfectly well, is wholesome for him, whilst it continues to do so whenever natural appetite calls for food."

Celsus spoke very right when he said that a healthy man ought not to tie himself up by strict rules, nor to abstain from any sort of food; that he ought sometimes to fast, and sometimes to feast. When applied to eating, nothing is more true than the proverb—

"Bonarum rerum consuetudo pessima est.—SYRUS.

"The too constant use, even of good things, is hurtful."

It is certainly better to restrain ourselves, so as to *use*, but not to *abuse*, our enjoyments; and to this we may add the opinion of doctor Fothergil, which the experience of every individual confirms, namely, that "the food we fancy most, sits easiest on the stomach."

What has been so far stated on the choice and quantity of food to be taken at a time, of course, relates only to persons in a state of health; the diet of the delicate, the sickly, and the infirm, must be regulated by the physician, and even the aged require particular kinds of food.

"Experience[17] has fully convinced me, (says an eminent Physiologist), that the latter stages of human life, are often abridged by unsuitable diet."

[17] Carlisle on the disorders of Old Age, ps. 2 and 27. This book exhibits an excellent view of the most suitable diet for aged, weak, and sickly people.

"The most numerous tribe of disorders incident to advanced life, spring from the failure or errors of the stomach, and its dependancies, and perhaps the first sources of all the infirmities of inability, may be traced to effects arising from imperfectly digested food."

EXTRAORDINARY GREAT EATERS, AND OBSERVATIONS ON ABSTINENCE.

In some persons, an extraordinary great appetite seems to be constitutional.

Charles Domery, aged 21 years, when a prisoner of war, at Liverpool, consumed in one day

	4lbs.	of Raw Cow's Udder.
	10lbs.	Raw Beef.
	2lbs.	Tallow Candles.
Total	16lbs.	

and five bottles of porter; and although allowed the daily rations of ten men, he was not satisfied.

Another extraordinary instance has been recorded by Baron Percy:—A soldier of the name of *Tarare*, who, at the age of 17, could devour in the course of 24 hours, a leg of beef weighing 24lbs. and thought nothing of swallowing the dinner dressed for fifteen German peasants. But those men were remarkable not only for the quantity of food they consumed, but also for its quality, giving a preference to raw meat, and even living flesh and blood.

Domery, in one year, eat 174 cats, dead and alive; and *Tarare* was strongly suspected of having eaten an infant.

Man can sustain the privation of food for several days, more or fewer in number, according to circumstances—the old better than the young, and the fat better than the lean. The absolute want of drink can be suffered only a short time, they have been strikingly described by Mungo Park and Ali Bey, as experienced in their own persons.

The narratives of ship-wrecked mariners also prove, with how very little food life may be supported for a considerable length of time; and the history of those impostors who pretend to live altogether without food or drink, display this adaptation of the wants of the body to its means of supply in a still more striking manner; for, even after the deception, in such cases as that of Ann Moore, is exposed, it will be found that the quantity of aliment actually taken was incredibly small.

Captain Woodard has added to his interesting narrative many instances of the power of the human body to resist the effects of severe abstinence. He himself and his five companions rowed their boat for seven days without any sustenance but a bottle of brandy, and then wandered about the shores of Celebes six more, without any other food than a little water and a few berries. Robert Scotney lived seventy-five days alone in a boat with three pounds and a half of meat, three pounds of flour, two hogsheads of water, some whale oil, and a small quantity of salt. He also used an amazing quantity of tobacco. Six soldiers deserted from St. Helena in a boat, on the 10th of June 1799, with twenty-five pounds of bread and about thirteen gallons of water. On the 18th, they reduced their allowance to one ounce of bread and two mouthfuls of water, on which they subsisted till the 26th, when their store was expended. Captain Inglefield, with eleven others, after five days of scanty diet, were obliged to restrict it to a biscuit divided into twelve morsels for breakfast, and the same for dinner, with an ounce or two of water daily. In ten days, a very stout man died, unable to swallow, and delirious. Lieutenant Bligh and his crew lived forty-two days upon five day's provisions.

In the tenth volume of Hufland's *Journal*, is related a very remarkable, and well-authenticated case of voluntary starvation. A recruit, to avoid serving, had cut off the fore-finger of his right hand. When in hospital for the cure of the wound, dreading the punishment which awaited him, he resolved to starve himself; and on the 2nd of August began obstinately to refuse all food or drink, and persisted in this resolution to the 24th of August. During these twenty-two days he had absolutely taken neither food, drink, nor medicine, and had no evacuation from his bowels. He had now become very much emaciated, his belly somewhat distended, he had a violent pain in his loins, his thirst was excessive, and his febrile heat burning. His behaviour had also become timid. Having been promised his discharge, unpunished, he was prevailed upon to take some sustenance, but could not, at first, bear even weak soup and luke-warm drinks. Under proper treatment, he continued to mend for eight days, and his strength was returning, when, on the 1st of September, he again refused food and got a wild look. He took a little barley-water every four or five days to the 8th; from that day to the 11th, he took a little biscuit with wine; but again from the 11th September to the 9th October, a period of twenty-eight days, he neither took food, drink, nor had any natural evacuation. From the 9th to the 11th he again took a little nourishment, and began to recruit; but, on the 11th, he finally renewed his resolution to starve himself, and persevered until his death, which took place on the 21st November, after a total abstinence of 42 days.

REMARKS ON THE ORIGIN OF THE CUSTOM OF EATING FLESH.

We are told, that in the first ages of the world, men lived upon acorns, berries, and such fruits as the earth spontaneously produced, and that in the Shepherd state of society, milk, obtained from flocks and herds, came into use. Soon afterwards the flesh of wild animals was added to the food, and the juice of grape to the drink of the human species. Hogs were the first animals, of the domestic kind, that were eaten by men, for they held it ungrateful to eat the animals that assisted them in their labour. "We are happy to find, (says the author of an elegant poem[18]) that it was not on account of the solidity, wholesomeness, delicacy, and other excellent qualities of his flesh, that the ox was worshipped on the banks of the Nile, and in the gorgeous temples of Memphis; for, although professedly friends to gastronomy, moderated by a decided aversion to any thing like sensuality, we are of opinion that man is less fit to feed upon *carnal* than vegetable substance."

[18] Tabella Cibaria, p. 33.

"The noble horse, fierce and unsubdued, was still roaming with all the roughness and intractability of original freedom, in his native groves, who already domesticated, the honest steer had willingly lent the strength of his powerful shoulders to the laborious strife of the plough. This had not only raised altars to him under the name of APIS, but even placed him among the first constellations of the Zodiac above the watchful eyes of the Chaldeans. In the reign of Erichtonius, fourth king of Athens, Diomus was offering to Jupiter the first fruits of the earth. Whilst the priests were busied apart in preparing some necessaries to the solemnity, an ox, passing by, browsed of all that had been gathered on the altar for the sacrifice. Diomus, in his disappointment and passion, slew him on the spot. The Gods, instead of countenancing his religious zeal, sent forth immediately all the horrors of a pestilence upon the Athenians, which did not cease until they had instituted a festival called *"The Death of the Ox."*[19]

[19] Nonius de re Cibaria.

"Porphyrius traces the custom of eating meat to *Pygmalion,* king of Tyre, in Phœnicia. Although the Jews were allowed to eat the flesh of the immolated beasts, in the golden age, man had not found courage and appetite enough to eat the flesh of an innocent animal; but soon after, this cruelty extended to nearly all quadrupeds, except those who were carnivorous. Tradition states, that *Prometheus* was the first who killed a bullock, *Ceres* a pig, and *Bacchus* a goat, for the uses of their tables. It is obvious that pigs, by turning up the new-sown fields for the sake of the grain, and goats browzing the tender sprouts of the vine-tree, were respectively inimical to *Ceres* and *Bacchus*. As for the killing of the first bullock by *Prometheus*, we leave to other commentators to explain."

COMPARATIVE ALIMENTARY EFFECTS OF ANIMAL AND VEGETABLE FOOD.

Animal food alone is ill adapted to form the whole of our aliment. The inquiries of physiologists have determined, that animal food is highly stimulant, and like all other stimulants, after the excitement has been brought to its acmé, debility must by necessity succeed. This, however, is not so much the case where fresh meat is used as when the meat is salted; but this may be, because our examples, with regard to fresh meat, are less marked than in the case of salted provision. For few instances occur in which fresh meat forms the whole food, exclusive altogether of fruits or other vegetable aliment. Salted meat often constitutes a great proportion of the food in long sea voyages, in the long dreary winters in Lapland, and amongst the inhabitants of besieged towns.

When this practice is continued for any length of time, oppression and langour begin to be felt, indigestion is brought on, and hurried breathing and a quick pulse on taking the slightest exercise, the gums become soft and spongy, the breath becomes fœtid, and the limbs swoln. Such are the dreadful effects produced by salted provisions, when a proper proportion of vegetable food is not used along with them.

The fact is, that nations, whose food is entirely vegetable, are less active and energetic than those whose diet is more nutritive. The inhabitants of Ireland, in the most humble walks of life, for example, who live almost exclusively on potatoes, are said to be more indolent and sluggish, when compared with their neighbours in England, who would think such diet to be no better than a prison allowance of bread and water.

In the East, where rice forms the great article of food with some tribes, the people are far from being robust or able to undergo much fatigue in labour or in war. The striking fact, that the English soldiers and sailors surpass all those of other nations in bravery and hardihood, is sufficient, we think, to demonstrate the effect of a considerable proportion of animal food. —For, though it be said, that a great number of our soldiers are Irishmen, yet our argument holds good, since, all these when in the army, or navy, live exactly in the same manner as the English themselves. The change of diet, indeed, is in these brave men very obvious; for the Irish and Scots soldiers are often more hardy than the English; not as it is supposed because they have been innured to greater hardships in their youth, but because their diet being more generous than it was at that period, its effects become more obvious than in those who have always had animal food.

When we examine the structure of the digestive organs of the inferior animals which live wholly on vegetable food, we find that they are very differently constituted from man, and much more so from the animals of prey. If the organs for digestion of the ruminant animals are more complicated, it should seem to follow, that vegetable aliment is more difficult to digest; otherwise, nature, who never works in vain, would not have provided for them such a series of stomachs. Hence we infer, that since man has not this apparatus peculiar to ruminant animals, it must be plain that nature did not intend him to live exclusively on vegetables. If we consider the human teeth, we shall be led to the same conclusion, for they are not either like the teeth of ruminant animals or those of beasts of prey, but intermediate between the two. We have *incisor* teeth like animals of the order glires: such as the hare, the rabbit, and the guinea-pig; *canin* teeth like those of the order feræ: such as the dog, the tiger, and the lion; and *grinders*, like herbivorous quadrupeds: such as the horse, the sheep, and the cow.

Food, then, composed of animal and vegetable substances, seems to be the best adapted for our organs of mastication and digestion, though it would not be easy to say precisely what proportions of these are most agreeable to the intentions of nature. We may safely conclude, however, that the vegetable food ought to exceed the animal in quantity. The direction given by Dr. Fothergill is the most judicious we have met with. "I have only" says he "one short caution to give. Those who think it necessary to pay any attention to their health at table, should take care that the quantity of bread, of meat, of pudding, and of greens, should not compose each of them a meal, as if some were only thrown in to make weight; but they should carefully observe, that the sum of all together do not exceed due bounds, or encroach upon the first feeling of satiety."

OBSERVATIONS ON THE VARIOUS KINDS OF ANIMAL SUBSTANCES COMMONLY USED FOR FOOD.

Of the different classes of animals used for food, quadrupeds compose the greatest proportion, and there is no part of their bodies which does not contain nutritive parts, and that has not been used as food in some way or other. Even bones affords an alimentary jelly fit for human food.

The largest portion of our aliment, however, is derived from the voluntary muscles of animals, or what is more strictly called, the flesh, consisting of all the red fibrous substance which covers the bones. It should seem that this is both the most nourishing and the most easily digested of animal substances. The red colour arises from the blood of minute vessels which run in every direction among the fibres; but whether this is the cause of the red muscle being more nutritious is not well ascertained. Thence the flesh of quadrupeds is more largely consumed than of any other class of animals; and, indeed, those in common use in most parts of Europe possesses all the alimentary properties in the highest perfection. All animal flesh seems more or less stimulating; and, in general, the more so the darker its colour is—but it does not absolutely follow that it is also more nutritious.

There is a considerable difference in the qualities of muscular flesh, according to the size of the animal, and also according to its activity. The small mountain sheep, for example, which has to encounter fatigue to procure its food, has flesh of a different quality and flavour from the large and lazy creature, which feeds luxuriously and fattens rapidly, in the rich pastures of the plain country. The beef of the western islands also, is more esteemed, on account of the same circumstance, than that of the fat and brawny oxen which we see in the London market. It is for this reason, we have no doubt, that the flesh of the horse, the rhinocerus, and elephant, is not used as food except in cases when other food is not to be procured. In the circumstance of activity altering the qualities of flesh, we may be allowed to instance the superiority of venison to beef, in flavour and tenderness, and easiness of digestion.

The age of animals is another circumstance which has great influence on the qualities of their flesh. The flesh of young animals is composed of less rigid fibres, and has fewer vessels which carry red blood running through it, and besides, it has less of the peculiar flavour of its particular species than the flesh of older animals. Gelatine is more abundant in the young, and fibrin in the old; hence the former is more bland and tender. Veal and lamb, for example, are more tender and gelatinous than beef or mutton; sucking pigs, chickens, and ducklings, are also much more delicate than the grown animals. The beef of an old cow, however well fed, is quite tough and unpalatable, while that of a very young heifer is much relished. Although, however, very young animals be so much more tender, yet they are insipid and flabby.

In the case of pork, age is not required, as in other sorts of butcher meat, to mellow the fibre. It is an aliment containing much nourishment; but to some palates its flavour is disagreeable, though by most people it is relished. It was much used by the ancient athletæ, as half raw beef steaks are now by our men of the fancy.

Sucking pigs are killed when three weeks old; and for pork, pigs are killed from six to twelve months old. It requires them to be older for making brawn. The flesh of young venison is not so good as when four years old or more; though that of the fawn is very tender and succulent.

But even in the fœtal state, the flesh of animals, if recently taken from a healthy mother, may be used. In the London market the fœtus of the cow is regularly sold to the pastry-cooks for the purpose of making mock turtle soup, of which it often forms the principal portion.

Veal, however, is reckoned not so good when killed before it be eight or ten weeks old. The most remarkable quality of flesh of this kind is, its almost wholly dissolving in boiling water, forming in the warm state a bland and gelatinous soup, and when cold, concreting into a tremulous transparent jelly. It is less animalized, or more properly speaking, contains less animal fibre than almost any other flesh; hence its tendency to become ascescent when made into broth and jelly, which is not the case with beef or mutton broth. The parts of older animals, which contain a larger portion of gelatine, are in this respect similar to young flesh. Cow-heel and sheep's-head are well known instances. It may be remarked that such food is less nutritious, and unless very much boiled, is less digestible than muscular flesh; but as it is also more light and less stimulating, it is frequently given to delicate people who cannot take any thing stronger.

Tripe is intermediate between what we have just described and the muscular flesh of grown animals, insomuch as there is in the stomach of ruminant animals a considerable proportion of vessels, transmitting red blood, and of muscular fibres, and accordingly it is to be inferred that tripe is more nutritive; it is certain it is more palatable and savory.

As to other parts of animals, which are abundantly furnished with red blood, though destitute of muscle, we cannot speak so decidedly. Some of the glands are coarse and rank flavoured, from the peculiar secretions which they produce, and are only used by poor persons; others are esteemed as delicacies, and seem not to be unwholesome. As examples of the latter, we may mention *sweet bread* or *pancreas,* one of the glands belonging to the digestive organs; and the liver of some species of birds, and of young quadrupeds.

The liver of the goose reckoned a great delicacy in Sicily, and they have there a a method of enlarging this organ while the bird is alive, but it is so cruel, that Brydon, who mentions it, declines giving the particulars, lest our epicures in England should have the inhumanity to give it a trial. The spleen is an instance of the former case, being strongly ill flavoured.

Another circumstance which produces difference of quality in flesh, is the sex of the animal, the genital organs having in this respect a very remarkable influence, as appears from the effect of destroying these by castration. This renders the flesh of the male similar, and in some cases, as in mutton, superior to that of the female, which is always more tender, and of finer fibre than that of the uncastrated male. By destroying also the ovaries of the females, their flesh is rendered more delicate, though this operation is not often practised. The sow is the animal which is most usually operated upon with this view; the flesh of the uncastrated boar is very coarse and bad. Even in calves the difference is observable, and veal is greatly improved by castrating the males. The same practice greatly improves fowl, as in capons. Venison is rank, tough, lean, and ill flavoured, and not fit to be eaten when killed during the rutting season, in September and October; and salmon, when about to spawn, are also bad, and prohibited, we believe, by our laws, to be caught or sold.

The mode of feeding animals, designed for the table, has also great influence on the quality of the flesh, so much so, that nice judges can distinguish whether mutton, if from the same breed of sheep, has been fed on grass or on turnips; and can tell, still more accurately, on tasting the fat of pork, whether the pigs have been fed on sour skimmed milk, brewers grains, or pease flour. It was the practice sometime ago, but now almost laid aside, to feed calves and oxen on oil cake. This did certainly fatten them, but the fat was rather rancid in most cases, and never of good flavour. The truth seems to be, that, though generally, the lean of fat animals is the most tender and palatable, yet that this is not so much the case when the fat is rapidly produced by artificial management in the feeding.

Sheep become very rapidly fat in the first stage of the rot, in consequence, perhaps, of their desire for food being greatly increased by the disease; and, taking advantage of this, it is said that some butchers are in the practice of producing rot artificially, which is certainly very blameable. Some amateurs of mutton are fond of such as has died of a sort of colic, called in the North *braxy*, that produces a very peculiar flavour in the meat, which is always, however, roasted, and never stewed or boiled. Such tastes are, to say the least of them, surely unnatural.

It is, perhaps, owing to the different quality and quantity of food, as much as any thing, that the season of the year has an effect upon the flesh of animals; the heat or cold of the weather, and in some cases, the periodical return of sexual attachment, must also be taken int to be out of seasono account. In the instances of veal and lamb, the words, *in season, and out of season*, refer, perhaps, more to plenty and scarceness than to any quality in the meat; for as soon as any thing is so plentiful in the market as to cause a fall in the price, and bring it within reach of the poor, then the wealthy classes pronounce it to be *out of season*.

This is the case with some sorts of birds which migrate at certain times of the year, the woodcock for example, and are on that account to be valued when they can be procured. Such as breed here, the solan goose for example, can be procured in the young state before they take their flight to their unknown retreat.

It has been roundly asserted, that there is no bird, and no part of any birds, which may not be safely used as food. Many species, however, are very oily, tough, or bad flavoured, and it is not at least very desirable to eat any animal which feeds on prey or carrion; even though this did not, as it does, taint their flesh. The qualities of the flesh of birds differ very much, both in the several species, and in particular parts of the same bird.

The flesh of birds which live on grain, is for the most part preferred to those which feed on insects or fish.

The pheasant, the turkey, as well as partridge, and moor game, are more esteemed than goose, duck, or woodcock.

Many of the water birds, however, are preferred, though from the nature of their food, they are apt to taste strongly of fish, and to become too fat and oily: to remedy these defects, skilful cooks sometimes bury them under ground for some days, and carefully remove all the skin, and as much as possible of the fat and oil from the inside, before dressing them.

Of the several sorts of birds, those of larger size are coarser and more tough than the smaller sorts; bustards, and larks, and ortolans, for example, than swans, or turkeys, and geese. This difference is also rendered greater in proportion to their age.

With regard to the particular parts of the same birds, the flesh of the wing, and the part of the breast nearest the wing, consisting of the muscles exerted in flying, are more dry, tender, and of a whiter colour than the muscles of the leg. This, however, is not the case with black game, in which the more superficial of these muscles are dark-coloured, while those deeper seated are pale; and the same is sometimes seen in other birds. The belly and the muscles of the thigh, when young enough, or when long kept and properly cooked, are both palatable, juicy, and sufficiently tender. The tendons of these muscles, however, are very tough, and at a certain age become cartilaginous and even bony.

Birds in a domestic state do not readily become fat, if allowed to go at large; for this purpose, they should be confined in coops, and supplied with as much wholesome food as they can eat. Poulterers even cram them with food. Domestic water fowls, must, while fattening, be kept from the water, otherwise they will acquire a strong fishy taste, and besides, will always remain lean. In general, over fatness may be considered as a sort of oleagenous dropsy, and seldom or never is met with in a state of nature.

All the soft parts of fish contain gelatine and fibrous substance, and are, consequently, in the edible sorts, nutritious. The fibrous portions are not, except in a few species, red, like the muscular flesh of land animals, but white and opake when dressed. If cooked fish looks bluish and semi-transparent, it is not in season. It is fortunate for us, that few if any poisonous fish are found in our seas, being chiefly confined to the tropics.

The roe of the greater number of fishes is eaten: caviar is the roe of the sturgeon.

Cods sounds, or the swim bladder of the larger cod, are reckoned a great delicacy when properly preserved. It is not usual for the skin of any animal to be eaten, though the skin of some sorts of fish which are pulpy and gelatinous are relished—as the skin of calves head is used for mock turtle soup. The flavour of fish depends greatly on their food, which, it is supposed, is the main cause of the difference between fresh and salt water fish, and between the same sorts of fish taken in different lakes and rivers, and on different parts of the coast.

Some shell fish, such as muscles and cockles, are occasionally found to disagree with some particular constitutions, but it is not true that this arises from their feeding on copper banks; some say, that it is from the persons eating the beard or fibres, by which the muscles attach themselves to the rocks, which is not, we think, probable.

The limpet (*Patella vulgata*), the periwinkle (*turbo littoreus*) and whilk (*murex antiquus*), are used as food, boiled by the common people in various districts of this country.

The crustaceous shellfish of sufficient size, are very generally esculent. These chiefly belong to the family of *Cancer*. Hence, several species of crabs, both short and long tailed, are eaten. The lobster, the crawfish, the shrimp, and the prawn belong to this class.

OBSERVATIONS ON THE VARIOUS KINDS OF VEGETABLE SUBSTANCES COMMONLY USED FOR FOOD.

The vegetable substances used for food are, if we include fruits, much more numerous than those derived from the animal kingdom. The chief of these, however, are the different sorts of grain and pulse, the *farina* or flour of which, contains a large proportion of starch, gluten, and mucilage, and but little woody fibre, and is consequently highly nutritious, and easily digested. To this class of plants we are also indebted for the food of the animals whose flesh is most generally used. In pulse, as well as in rye and oats, there is, besides the principles just mentioned, a considerable portion of sugar, which adds to their nutritive qualities.

We would class the different sorts of nuts, next to grain and pulse, in the proportion of nutriment which they afford; starch and mucilage are their chief elements, but these are combined with a kind of oil which is not of easy digestion, and makes them disagree with most people when too liberally used. Almonds, filberts, walnuts, and cocoa, are the nuts in most request. Chocolate is a preparation of this kind, which is very nutritious to those with whom it agrees.

Next to grain, pulse, and nuts, we may place the farinaceous roots, potatoes, carrots, parsnips, and Jerusalem artichokes. Of these, the first, contains the most nourishment, which depends on the great proportion of starch with which it abounds. Other pot-herbs possess little nourishment.

Cabbage and greens, for example, are chiefly composed of fibre, mucilage, and water, and the same is true of onions, leeks, celery, lettuce, and broccoli.

Of fruits, those which are most farinaceous and mucilaginous, and which are sweet from the sugar contained in them, are the most nutritious. The pear should seem to answer this description the nearest, but experience proves that this fruit is of less easy digestion than the apple, whose greater acidity corrects the heavy quality of the saccharine matter with which the pear abounds.

GENERAL OPERATIONS OF COOKERY.

Few of the substances which we use for food are consumed in the state in which they are originally produced by nature. With the exception of some fruits and salads, all of them undergo some preparation. In most cases, indeed, this is indispensable; for, otherwise, they would not only be less wholesome and nutritive, but less digestible. The preceding observations, therefore, are only applicable to the materials when cooked, and not to the crude vegetables and raw flesh in the undressed state.

The general processes of cookery resolve themselves into the various modes of applying heat under different circumstances. They are the following—roasting, frying, broiling, baking, stewing, and boiling. These operations not only soften the raw materials, and render them alimentary, but the chemical constitution of the cooked substance suffers also such alterations, that its constituent parts can often no longer be recognised.

ROASTING ON A SPIT

Appears to be the most ancient process of rendering animal food eatable by means of the action of heat.

Spits were used very anciently in all parts of the world, and perhaps, before the plain practice of hanging the meat to a string before the fire. Ere the iron age had taught men the use of metals, these roasting instruments were made of wood; and as we find it in Virgil,[20] slender branches of the hazel tree were particularly chosen—

>   ———"Stabit sacer hircus ad aram
> "Pinguiaque in verubus torrebimus extra colurnis."
> The altar let the guilty goat approach,
> And roast his fat limbs on the hazel broach."
>
> [20] Georgics II. 545.

Roasting is the most simple and direct application of heat in the preparation of food. The process is, for the most part, confined to animal substances, though several fruits, such as apples, chesnuts, and some roots, are in this manner directly subjected to fire.

But in dressing animal food, butcher's meat, venison, fowl, and fish, roasting is one of the most usual processes, and it is, we believe, the best for rendering food nutritive and wholesome. The chemical changes also which roasting induces, are sufficiently slight, as a careful analysis will procure from meat, properly roasted, nearly all the elements which are to be found in it in the raw state. Slight as the change is however in a chemical, it is considerable in a culinary, point of view. The texture of the meat is more relaxed and consequently it is more tender; it is also more sapid and high flavoured. It is absolutely essential that the meat intended for roasting, has been kept long enough for the fibres to become flaccid, without which precaution the best meat does not become tender. If the meat be frozen, it should be thawed, by putting it into cold water, before it is put on the spit.

The process of roasting requires some care to conduct it properly. The meat should be gradually turned before the fire, in order to effect its uniform exposure to the rays of heat. A covering of paper prevents the fat from taking fire, and frequently *basting* the meat with gravy or melted fat, prevents it from being scorched or becoming dry, bitter, and unpalatable. It is necessary to be very careful in placing the meat to be roasted at a proper distance from the fire. If it is put too near, the surface will be scorched and burnt to a cinder, while the inner portion will be quite raw; and, if it be too distant, it will never have either the tenderness or the flavour it would have had by proper care. At first, it should be placed at some distance, and afterwards be gradually brought nearer the fire, to give the heat time to penetrate the whole piece equally; and, the larger the joint is, the more gradually should this be done. Poultry, in particular, should be heated very gradually.

When the joint is of an unequal thickness, the spit must be placed slanting, so that the thinnest part is further removed from the fire.

The less the spit is made to pass through the prime part of the meat, the better. Thus, in a shoulder of mutton, the spit is made to enter close to the shank-bone, and passed along the blade-bone of the joint.

When the meat is nearly sufficiently roasted, it is dusted over with a coating of flour; this, uniting with the fat and other juices exuded on the surface, covers the joint with a brown crust, glazed and frothy, which gives to the eye a prelude of the palatable substance it encrusts.

The process, as just described, is very similar, whatever may be the sort of meat roasted, whether joints, and the several species of fowl, or game. Fish is not usually dressed in this way, though the larger sorts are sometimes roasted. Those who relish eels and pike prefer them roasted to any other mode of dressing them.

It is a general practice to move the spit back when the meat is half done, in order to clear the bottom part of the grate, and to give the fire a good stirring, that it may burn bright during the remainder of the process. The meat is deemed sufficiently roasted when the steam puffs out of the joint in jets towards the fire.

To facilitate the process of roasting, a metal screen, consisting of a shallow concave reflector, is placed behind the meat, in order to reflect the rays of heat of the fire back again upon the meat. This greatly hastens the process. The screen is usually made of wood, lined with tin. It should be kept bright, otherwise, it will not reflect the rays of heat.

ROASTING ON A STRING

Is usually performed by means of the useful contrivance called a *bottle jack*, a well-known machine, so named from its form. It only serves for small joints, but does that better than the spit. It is cheap and simple, and the turning motion is produced by the twisting and untwisting of a string. The sort of roasting machine, called the *Poor Man's Spit*, is something of the same nature, but still more simple. The meat is suspended by a skein of worsted, a twirling motion being given to the meat, the thread is twisted, and when the force is spent, the string untwists itself two or three times alternately, till the action being discontinued, the meat must again get a twirl round. When the meat is half done, the lower extremity of the joint is turned uppermost, and affixed to the string, so that the gravy flows over the joint the reverse way it did before.

ROASTING IN AN OPEN OVEN.

A Dutch or open oven is a machine for roasting small joints, such as fowls, &c. It consists of an arched box of tin open on one side, which side is placed against the fire. The joint being either suspended in the machine on a spit, or by a hook, or put on a low trevet placed on the bottom of the oven, which is moveable. The inside of the oven should be kept bright that it may reflect the heat of the fire. This is the most economical and most expeditious method of roasting in the small way.

ROASTING IN A CLOSED OVEN.

Roasting in a closed oven, or *baking*, consists in exposing substances to be roasted to the action of heat in a confined space, or closed oven, which does not permit the free access of air, to cause the vapour arising from the roasted substance to escape as fast as it is formed, and this circumstance materially alters the flavour of roasted animal substances.

Roasters and ovens of the common construction are apt to give the meat a disagreeable flavour, arising from the empyreumatic oil, which is formed by the decomposition of the fat, exposed to the bottom of the oven. This inconvenience has been completely remedied in two ways, by providing against the evil of allowing the fat to burn; and secondly, by carrying out of the oven by a strong current of heated air, the empyreumatic vapours, as fast as they are formed.

Such are the different processes of roasting meat.

Rationale.—The first effect of the fire is to rarify the watery juices within its influence which make their escape in the form of steam. The albuminous portion then coagulates in the same manner as the white of an egg does, the gelatine and the osmazome[21] become detached from the fibrine, and unite with a portion of the fat, which also is liquified by the expansive property of heat. The union of these form a compound fluid not to be found in the meat previously. This is retained in the interstices of the fibres where it is formed by the brown frothy crust, but flows abundantly from every pore when a cut is made into the meat with a knife. In consequence of the dissipation of the watery juices, the fibrous portion becomes gradually corrugated, and, if not attentively watched, its texture is destroyed, and it becomes rigid. Chemists prove that the peculiar odour and taste of roasted meat depends on the development of the principle which has been called *osmazome*, or the *animal extractive matter* of the old chemist, a substance which differs very much from every other constituent part of animal matter *chemically,* in being soluble in alcohol—and to the *senses,* in being extremely savoury or sapid. It is upon this principle, which seems to admit of considerable varieties, that the peculiar grateful flavour of animal food, (whether in the form of broth or roasted,) and of each of its kinds, depends. Osmazome exists in the largest quantity in the fibrous organs, or combined with fibrine in the muscles, while the tendons and other gelatinous organs appear to be destitute of it. The flesh of game, and old animals, contains it in greater quantity than that of young animals abounding in gelatine.

[21] Derived from οσμη, *smell,* and ζωμος, *broth.*

The tenderness produced by roasting, we account for, from the expansion of the watery juices into steam, loosening and dissevering the fibres one from another, in forcing a passage through the pores to make their escape by. This violence, also, must rupture all the finer network of the cellular membranes, besides the smaller nerves and blood vessels which ramify so numerously through every hair's-breadth of animal substance. This dissolution of all the minute parts of the meat, which must take place before a particle of steam can escape, will most clearly account both for the tenderness and the altered colour of roasted meat. The action of heat, also, upon the more solid parts of the bundles of fibres, will, independent of the expansion of the juices, cause them to enlarge their volume, and consequently make the smaller fibres less firmly adhesive.

BROILING.

Another process in which meat is subjected to the immediate action of fire is broiling, which at first sight seems not to differ from roasting. The effect on the meat is, however, considerably different. The process consists in laying chops or slices of meat on clear burning coals, or a gridiron placed over a clear fire. It is indispensable that the chops or slices be moderately thin, otherwise the outside will be scorched to a cinder before they are cooked within; from one fourth to three fourths of an inch is a proper thickness.[22] It is also necessary that the fire be moderately brisk, without smoke or flame, lest the meat should acquire a smoky taste. When a gridiron is used it ought to be thoroughly heated before the slices or chops are laid on it, to prevent them from sticking to the bars. In order to broil them equally, they must be turned from time to time till the cook can easily pierce them with a fork or sharp skewer, which is the test of them being sufficiently cooked. It is improper, however, to cut into the chops to ascertain whether they are broiled enough, because it lets out the gravy.

[22] It is recommended by cooks to previously beat the raw slices with a mallet, but this practice is a bad one.

Coke is the best fuel for broiling, for it does not emit any smoke, and gives a clear and moderate heat; a mixture of coke and charcoal is exceedingly well calculated for the broiling process.

Those gridirons of the usual appearance and form, that have the bars fluted or hollowed on the upper side, by which means, the fat that comes from the meat that is cooked on them, is prevented from falling into the fire, and causing flame and smoke are the best; for all the grease that runs down the bars is received into a small trough, which prevents it from being wasted or lost. The upright gridiron is a still better invention, as the meat cooked on it, is entirely free from smoke, and the melted fat is still more easily saved, and kept more clean.

Rationale.—The heat being very quickly and directly applied, not gradually as in roasting and baking, the surface of the meat is speedily freed from its watery juices, and the fibres become corrugated, forming a firm and crisp incrustation of fibre and fat. This crust effectually prevents the escape of the juices from within; namely, the gelatine, and the osmazome, which are more rapidly expanded by the heat than in roasting, and consequently must more violently dissever the small fibres among which they are lodged, the effect, however, is more mechanical than chemical, for it does not appear that any new combination is formed, nor much disorganization produced. Accordingly, it is found that broiled meat is more sapid, and contains more liquid albumen, gelatine, and free osmazome, than the same meat would do if boiled or roasted. It is this greater degree of juicyness, sapidity, and tenderness, that constitutes the peculiarity and perfection of this mode of cooking, compared with roasting, baking, or frying in a pan.

Every sort of meat, however, is not fit for broiling. The chemistry of the process will point out the sorts best adapted for it. The flesh, for example, of old animals, which is deficient in gelatine and albumen, would be too much dried by roasting. The larger muscles, also, which abound in fibrous substance, such as the rump of beef, are well fitted for broiling. The flesh of game is likewise less juicy and gelatinous, and forms a very savoury dish when broiled. The process is peculiarly fit for most sorts of fish, which roasting or baking would render dry and shrivelled, and in many cases boiling would make it too soft and pulpy. Fresh caught char, and trout,[23] are in the highest perfection when dressed in this way.

> [23] The best way of eating mackerel, is to broil it in buttered paper upon the gridiron; and, when properly done, to put fresh butter in the inside, with chopped parsley, pepper, and salt, which melts, and adds an exceedingly good flavour to the fish.

On the other hand, the flesh which abounds in watery juices and gelatine is not well adapted for broiling. The flesh of all young animals is of this kind; and accordingly lamb, veal, and sucking pig; the flesh of the fawn and kid do not answer to be broiled but roasted. The same is true of all the parts of an animal, whatever be its age, which abound more in gelatine, albumen, and fat, than in red muscular fibre.

Broiled beef steaks were the established breakfast of the Maids of Honour of Queen Elizabeth. At an earlier period they gave strength and vigour to those who

"————————————————drew,
"*And almost joined the horns* of the tough yew."

FRYING.

Frying is a process somewhat intermediate between roasting and boiling. Indeed, in one sense, it may be termed boiling, as it is the application of heat to the substance to be cooked, through the medium of melted fat, raised to the boiling temperature. The effect on the meat is very peculiar, and easily distinguished from every other mode of cooking. The meat is prepared in the same way as in broiling, by cutting it into chops, or slices, of not more than half an inch or three quarters in thickness. A sufficient quantity of mutton or beef suet, butter, lard, or oil, being melted in a pan, and made boiling-hot, the meat is laid in it. It is not necessary that the meat be *wholly* immersed in the boiling fat; if it be immersed in part, it will be quite sufficient. When flesh is the substance to be fried, the pieces, previously to their being put into the pan, are sometimes brushed over with eggs and crumbs of stale bread, flour, or any other farinaceous substance. This application may also be made when the meat is nearly cooked. The intention of it is to cover the meat with a thin brown crust, the savour of which increases the relish of the dish. Fish are, for the most part, treated in this manner when fried. It answers well with trout, whitings, flounders, and soles. When this application is made to the meat previously to its being put into the pan, the peculiar flavour of the meat is more effectually retained. One of the best preparations for this purpose is oatmeal, flour, or crumbs of stale bread, made into a liquid paste with the yolk and white of eggs.

Vegetable, as well as animal substances, are subjected to this process, though it is always at the expense of their wholesome and nutritive qualities; and not always to the improvement of their taste and flavour.

As in the case of animal substances, all the juices are, by frying, extracted from the vegetables; with this difference, however, that their place is not supplied by the melted fat; for the starch of the vegetables (potatoes for example) is rendered insoluble in water by the fat, and exhibits a corneous appearance and texture. Fried potatoes are the most familiar instance of the process. When cut into thin slices and fried in oil, butter, or lard, they are rendered semi-transparent. Cabbage, or the stalks, leaves, and fruits of other vegetable substances, previously boiled and then fried, shrink, and become more easy to break, in proportion as the water is driven off from them, as this, during their previous boiling, dissolves the saccharine and amylaceous matter which rendered them supple and juicy. These principles are much better prepared and improved by boiling; they are very much deteriorated by the boiling fat in the frying pan.

The melted fat, or oil, should always be brought to the boiling point, or nearly so. The proper temperature is ascertained by putting into the fat a few sprigs of parsley, a thin slice of turnip, or a piece of bread, and if any of these substances become crisp without acquiring a black colour, the fat is hot enough for frying; if it be made hotter, it becomes blackened, and the meat acquires a burnt and unpleasant flavour. Any sort of hard fat, such as beef suet, is the best fitted for frying meat; because, fat of this description can be brought to a higher temperature, without suffering decomposition, than either lard, butter, or oil. There are, however, particular kinds of meat which answer better with some one or other of these than with any of the rest. Fish, for example, is best fried in oil.

A rich brown colour is communicated to the fried substance, by pressing it, when nearly cooked, against the bottom of the pan.

The fire for frying should be kept sharp and clear, to keep the melted fat at a sufficient high temperature, and without this precaution the fried substance cannot be browned. If the temperature of the fat is not hot enough, the fried meat will be sodden. Fish cannot be fried of a good colour, and crisp, and firm texture, unless the fat is boiling hot.

Frying, though one of the most common culinary occupations, is one of those that is least commonly performed.

Eggs are often fryed.

"Fresh butter, hissing in the pan, receives the yolk and white together in its burning bosom. One minute or two and all the noise is over; and, sprinkled with pepper, salt, and a few drops of vinegar, they appear perfectly fit for the table. The *salamander* is often held over them, and accelerates the culinary process."

Rationale.—The process of frying is considerably different from those which we have formerly been examining. In frying, the high temperature of the melted fat has the effect of extracting (at least from the outer surface) all the gelatine, osmazome and albumen, the place of which is, in part, supplied by the melted fat entering between the fibres, and gradually filling up the interstices. It is this circumstance which prevents the fibres of fried meat from becoming hard and dry, and preserves them in a tender and supple state. Meat which has been fried, shrinks more in bulk than when boiled or roasted, in consequence of the melted fat having a stronger influence in dislodging the animal juices. It is this also which gives the meat the structure which has not unaptly been compared to leather.

Taste informs us, independently of our *rationale*, that fried meat is less gelatinous and less savoury than when simply boiled or roasted. It is also less tender. The gelatine and other juices of the animal fibre, which are extracted during the process may be discovered, after the melted matter in the pan is suffered to settle, in the form of a rich, brown, savoury jelly, which separates spontaneously from the rest of the substance.

STEWING.

Stewing differs from roasting and broiling, in the heat being applied to the substance through a small portion of a liquid medium; and, from boiling and frying, in the process being conducted by means of an *aqueous*, and not by means of an oily fluid. It is necessary that the fire be moderate; for a strong heat suddenly applied would be very injurious. The liquids employed as the medium for applying the heat are usually water, gravy, or broth, the quantity of which must be such as shall prevent the meat from burning and adhering to the pan. It is not requisite that the liquid be made to boil in stewing. It should only be raised nearly to a simmering heat, which will retard the fluid being evaporated too quickly. The closeness of the vessel will also prevent the waste of the liquid. If it diminish too quickly, it must, from time to time, be replenished.

The management of the fire in cooking, is, in all cases, a matter of importance, but in no case is it so necessary to be attended to as in preparing stews or made dishes; not only the palatableness, but even the strength or richness of all made dishes, seems to depend very much upon the management of the heat employed in cooking them.

The most proper sorts of animal food for stewing, are such as abound in fibrine, and which are too dry or too tough for roasting. When beef or mutton is rather old and too coarse flavoured, and not tender enough for the spit or the gridiron, it may, by stewing, be not only rendered tolerably palatable, but even sometimes savoury and good. But the stewing process is not confined to flesh of this sort; for veal and other young flesh which abounds in gelatine, when properly stewed, is much relished.

The vegetables most usually stewed are carrots, turnips, potatoes, pease, beans, and other leguminous seeds. Some fruits are also cooked in this way.

Rationale.—Stewing is nothing else than boiling by means of a small quantity of an aqueous fluid, and continuing the operation for a long time to render the substance tender, to loosen its texture, to render it more sapid, and to retain and concentrate the most essential parts of animal or vegetable food.

If the stew-pan be close shut, it is evident that none of the nutritive principles can escape, and must either be found in the meat itself or in the liquid. The water or gravy in which the meat is stewed, being capable of dissolving the gelatine and albumen, the greater part of them become separated during the simmering process. Now, since the firm texture of the bundles of fibres of the meat is owing to the solid gelatine and albumen glueing them, as it were, together, when they are dissolved and disengaged, the meat must become greatly disorganized. These principles, as well as the fat and osmazome, are partly disengaged from the meat, and become united with the gravy. It is to these, indeed, that the gravy owes all its richness and excellence. The muscular fibres and the tendons acquire a gluey appearance and texture, and the whole forms a savoury gelatinous *stew*, *gravy*, or *soup*.

No scorching or browning of the meat takes place if the process is properly conducted; for the temperature to which it is exposed does not exceed the boiling point of water.

In the stewing of vegetables, saccharine matter is formed, the starch and mucilage are rendered soluble, and of course, set free the woody fibre, which either floats through the liquid or adheres together very slightly. It accordingly constitutes either a pasty fluid, or converts the vegetables to a soft pulp; sometimes their original shape being preserved entire, and at other times not.

BOILING.

Boiling is a much more common operation than any of those we have considered, with the exception perhaps of roasting. It consists, as every body knows, in subjecting the materials of food to the influence of heat, through the medium of boiling water, or of steam.

The water employed for boiling meat or pulse should be soft, and the joint should be put on the fire immersed in cold water, in order that the heat may gradually cause the whole mass to become boiled equally.

If the piece of meat is of an unequal thickness, the thinner parts will be over-done before the more massy portion is sufficiently acted on by the boiling water.

Salted meat requires to be very slowly boiled, or simmered only, for a quick and rapid ebullition renders salted provisions extremely hard.

Frozen substances should be thoroughly thawed, and this is best effected by immersing them in cold water.

Count Rumford has taken much pains to impress on the minds of those who exercise the culinary art, the following simple but pratical, important fact, namely, that when water begins only to be agitated by the heat of the fire, it is incapable of being made hotter, and that the violent ebullition is nothing more than an unprofitable dissipation of the water, in the form of steam, and a considerable waste of fuel.

From the beginning of the process to the end of it the boiling should be as gentle as possible. Causing any thing to boil violently in any culinary process, is very ill-judged; for it not only does not expedite, in the smallest degree, the process of cooking, but it occasions a most enormous waste of fuel, and by driving away with the steam many of the more volatile and more savoury particles of the ingredients, renders the victuals less good and less palatable: it is not by the bubbling up, or *violent boiling*, as it is called, of the water that culinary operations are expedited.

One of the most essential conditions to be attended to in the boiling of meat is, to skim the pot well, and keep it really boiling, the slower the better. If the skimming be neglected, the coagulated albuminous matter will attach itself to the meat, and spoil the good appearance of it.

It is not necessary to wrap meat or poultry in a cloth, if the pot be carefully skimmed. The general rule of the best cooks is to allow from 20 to 30 minutes slow simmering to a pound of meat, reckoning from the time the pot begins to boil.

The cover of the boiling pot should fit close, to prevent the unnecessary evaporation of the water, and the smoke insinuating itself under the edge of the cover, and communicating to the boiled substance a smoky taste.

Cooks often put a trevet, or plate, on the bottom of the boiling pot, to prevent the boiled substance sticking to the pot.

Rationale.—When flesh or fish is boiled in an open vessel, or one not closely covered, the fibrous texture is rendered more tender: at the same time its nutritive quality is not much diminished. For the temperature of the water or steam, never exceeding 212°, is insufficient to produce the partial charring, which roasting and broiling effect. But, as in stewing, the gelatine, albumen, osmazome, and fat, are developed and disengaged, and becoming united with the liquid in the vessel, form a soup, or broth. The paler colour of boiled meat is owing to the blood being separated and diffused in the water. In frying, the boiling fat or oil enters into the interstices of the fibres, which the disengaged animal juices have left empty. In boiling, in a similar way, the hot water takes the place of the blood, gelatine, fat, and albumen, which have been dissolved and separated from the fibres. The fibres are in this manner soaked and washed, first by the boiling water, and afterwards by the soup or broth which is formed, till the whole texture assume a softened consistence, and pale appearance. It is this, rather than any softening of the fibres themselves, which seems to be the real effect produced, unless, with some, we consider the fibres as nothing more than minute and close-set bundles of blood vessels. This doctrine, however, the experience of every cook will disprove; for if the boiling be long continued, the fibres of the meat will alone remain, and so far from becoming more soft and pulpy, they will become dry and juiceless. If indeed the boiling point of the water be artificially increased above 212°, by pressure applied to the surface of the liquid, the fibres may be reduced to a pulp, quite homogeneous. When this is done by Papin's digester, or by any other apparatus of the same kind, and when the process under such circumstances is long continued, the hardest bones may be converted into jelly.

It is only by boiling that the more gelatinous parts of flesh can be completely extracted unaltered from such parts as are cartilaginous, ligamentous, or tendinous.

COMPARISON OF THE CHEMICAL CHANGES PRODUCED ON ANIMAL AND VEGETABLE FOOD, IN THE DIFFERENT PROCESSES OF COOKERY.

The principal operations of cookery which we have just examined and explained, all agree in this, that they effect some chemical change on the materials operated upon, by which they are rendered more digestible, more wholesome, and consequently more nutritive.

In such of the operations as are performed by the direct application of heat to the flesh of animals, namely, roasting, baking, frying, and broiling, the meat loses the vapid and nauseous taste and odour which it possesses in a raw state, and becomes savoury, juicy, and grateful to the taste. These effects arise from the development of the gelatine and osmazome from the smaller vessels, and their being rendered soluble; while, at the same time a portion of the fat is liquified, and combines with them after they are disengaged.

The fibres again, on the surface of the meat, are partly scorched, and form a crust, which, except in the interstices of the corrugations, is impermeable, and consequently prevents the savoury gravy that is disengaged from the fibres from oozing out or becoming evaporated. It is thus only disengaged from its chemical union with the fibres, and remains mechanically united with them in the meat, after it is cooked, as we see upon cutting into the fibrous portion.

The effect produced on the fat is somewhat different. The direct application of fire to this portion of the meat soon melts part of the substance, and raises it to the boiling point, or nearly so; the water which it contains is consequently given off in the form of steam, and it carries with it a quantity of osmazome. It is this which occasions the peculiar odour that arises from meat while roasting.

The vapid taste is also corrected by the empyreuma, combined with a minute quantity of ammonia, which is soon developed on the surface of the fat, by the partial charring—not of the fat itself, but of the cellular membrane in which it is enveloped. This structure may easily be perceived on a slight examination of a piece of recent fat; all the membranous or skinny portions being only the receptacles or nests for the fat itself. And since these membranes are for the most part exceedingly thin and easily ruptured, and since heat increases the volume of the fat which they contain, the application of heat in roasting or broiling will soon make all the membranes burst which are within its influence, and thus give a free passage for the juices to unite with each other.

There is, according to these statements, but little loss of the substance of meat when roasted or broiled, and the chemical changes produced are so slight, that nearly all its nutritive elements must be preserved and concentrated in the cooked meat.

When there is a watery medium used, through which heat is applied to animal food, as for example, in the process of stewing or boiling, a portion of the fat, gelatine, and osmazome, is dissolved, and mixes with the water. Nutritive matter is consequently lost, or, at least, it is transferred from the meat to the broth or soup.

In the operation of *stewing* there is less of this transfer made; and, besides, as the medium is scarcely kept at a boiling heat, less of the nutritive juices are dissolved. When, however, the broth or gravy in which meat is *boiled* is made use of, as well as the meat itself, boiling is the most economical practice; for though nothing be added except the water, this itself, if it contains no nourishment, at least fills the stomach, and serves to diffuse more widely the nutritive juices of the meat which it holds in solution or in mixture.

But though boiling be thus the most economical practice, it is not always to the taste of individuals, or even of whole nations to use the broth or soup. The English and Irish, for example, rarely follow this practice, while the Scots, French, and Germans, prefer it to all other modes of cooking. In general, then, it should seem, that roasting as it is the simplest, is also the best mode of rendering the flesh of animals fit for human food. Roasted meat is wholesome and highly nourishing; and when there is not too much of the empyreumatic crust formed, it is for the most part easily digested. In these respects, broiled meat differs little from such as is roasted. What is fried is always less tender. It is often found that roasted or broiled meat sits more easily on the stomach, and is sooner digested by those whose digestive organs are feeble or diseased, than fried or boiled meat, or broths and stews.

The effects of the processes of cookery on vegetable substances, though usually very slight and simple, are in some instances both striking and unexpected. For example, some sorts of vegetables are extremely acrid and even poisonous in their crude state, and altogether unfit for human food; yet, by simply boiling them in water, they become bland, sweet, and wholesome. Several species of *arum* (cuckoo-pint), which are very acrid, and would be dangerous to use raw, become quite palatable pot-herbs when boiled. Their acrimony must reside in a very volatile principle, which, during the boiling, makes its escape, or is chemically altered; but the nature of this principle has not yet been accurately investigated by chemists. A more familiar example than this is found in onions, leeks, and garlick, whose acrimony and strong odour can be almost destroyed, or rather driven off by a sufficiently long application of heat, either directly, or through the medium of water. Many other instances could be given, but we shall content ourselves with one more.

Every body knows that potatoes, in a raw state, are nauseous and unpalatable. It is not, perhaps, so generally known that the potatoe, (*solanum tuberosum*,) belongs to the night-shade genus of plants, which are all more or less poisonous. If potatoes were used raw, in any quantity, they would be deleterious to man; nor does it disprove this that cattle eat them with impunity, as sheep and goats eat plants much more strongly poisonous to man, such as hemlockdropwort, [*oenanthe crocata*;] and waterhemlock, [*phelandrium aquaticum*].

By boiling or roasting, however, all the unpalatable and all the unwholesome qualities of the potatoe are changed, and it becomes farinaceous, wholesome, digestible, and highly nutritious. Yet, although this change is remarkable, and could scarcely have been anticipated, very little is lost and nothing is added to the potatoe by either roasting or boiling, yet its immediate constituent parts have evidently suffered a very great chemical alteration, chiefly, in consequence it should seem, from the farinaceous substance being acted on by water.

Vegetables, when used as food, are most commonly boiled, and seldom baked or roasted. Salads, indeed, are eaten raw, without any application of heat. The chemical action of heat on pot-herbs, on esculent roots, and leguminous seeds, does not appear to be confined to the mere softening of their fibres, or to the solution or coagulation of some of their juices and component parts; for we have just now seen that their flavour, and other sensible qualities, as well as their texture, suffer a remarkable chemical change, which greatly improves their alimentary properties.

In the cooking of vegetables, saccharine matter is often formed, or mucilage and jelly extracted; and the whole substance is on that account rendered more palatable, wholesome, and nourishing. These effects are very well exemplified in the changes which take place in flour when converted into bread;[24] which differs materially from flour paste, insomuch that the constituent parts of the unbaked dough can no longer be separated by the processes employed in chemical analysis.

[24] A treatise on the *art* of making good and *wholesome* bread of wheat, oats, rye, barley, and other farinaceous grain, exhibiting the alimentary properties and chemical constitution of different kinds of bread corn, and of the various substitutes used for bread, in different parts of the world, p. 58, 1821.

Vegetable substances are most commonly boiled or baked; or, if occasionly fried or roasted, there is always much water present, which prevents the greater action of the fire from penetrating below the surface. The universal effect of cookery by boiling upon vegetable substances, is to dissolve in the water some of their constituents, such as the mucilage and starch, and to render those that are not properly soluble, as the gluten and fibre, softer and more pulpy.

COMPARATIVE DIMINUTION OF THE WEIGHT OF MEAT IN COOKING.

It is evident, that whether the heat be applied directly or indirectly for cooking animal food, there must be a considerable diminution of weight. In the cooking of animal substances in public institutions, where the allowance of meat is generally weighed out in its raw state, and includes bones, and is served out cooked, and sometimes without bone, it is a matter of importance to ascertain nearly their relative proportions. Much, no doubt, depends upon the piece of the meat cooked, and the degree of cookery, and the attention bestowed on it. Persons who salt rounds of beef to sell by retail, after it is boiled, get 19 lbs. of cold boiled beef from 25 lbs. raw; but the meat is always rather underdone.

Messrs. Donkin and Gamble boiled in steam 56 lbs. of captain's salt beef; the meat, when cold, without the bones, which amounted to 5 lbs. 6 oz. weighed only 35 lbs.

In another experiment, 113 lbs. of prime mess beef, gave 9 lbs. 10 oz. of bones, and 47 lbs. 8 oz. meat; and in a third, 213 lbs. mess beef gave 13 lbs. 8 oz. bones, and 103 lbs. 10 oz. meat; or, taken in the aggregate, 372 lbs. of salt beef, including bones, furnish, when boiled, 186 lbs. 2 oz., without bone, being about 50 *per cent.*; or, disregarding the bone altogether, salt meat loses, by boiling, about 44.2 per cwt. or nearly half.

We are indebted to Professor Wallace (of Edinburgh) for the detail of a very accurate and extensive experiment in a public establishment, of which the results were, that, in pieces of 10 lbs. weight, each 100 lbs. of BEEF lost, on an average, by *boiling*, 26.4; *baking*, 30.2; and *roasting*, 32.2: MUTTON, the leg, by *boiling*, 21.4; by *roasting* the shoulder, 31.1; the neck, 32.4; the loin, 35.9. Hence, generally speaking, *mutton* loses, by boiling, about one-fifth of its original weight, and *beef* about one-fourth; again, *mutton* and *beef* lose, by *roasting*, about one-third of their original weight.

The loss arises, in roasting, from the melting out of the fat and the evaporation of the watery part of the juices, but the nutritious matters remain condensed in the solid meat when cooked; but in boiling, the loss arises partly from fat melted out, but chiefly from gelatine and osmazome becoming dissolved in the water in which the meat is boiled; there is, therefore, a real loss of nutritive matter in boiling, unless the broth be used, when this mode of cooking becomes the most economical.

PRIMARY OR CHIEF DISHES OF THE ENGLISH TABLE.

The principal or chief dishes that are prepared for the English table, what the scientific cooks for the marshals and generals of France would term *dishes of the first order*, are few in number. *Flesh, fowl* and *fish*, roasted, boiled or fried, accompanied by some simple and easy made puddings and pies, are the primary dishes of an English table. Soups and broths are less generally made use of; and the flesh, fowl and fish, served up in made dishes, are, like the lord mayor in his state coach, generally less noticed than the attendants.

BROTH

May be defined a weak decoction of meat, slightly seasoned with the addition of aromatic herbs, roots or spices, in which the flavour of the meat greatly predominates.

To produce a high flavoured broth, it is essential that the boiling of the meat be moderate, and continued for some time; the simmering should be done in a vessel nearly closed. Cooks consider it essential that the broth be clear; the scum, or albumen of the meat, which becomes coagulated and rises to the surface during the boiling, must therefore be removed from time to time.

The meat employed for broth (and also for soup and gravy), should be fresh, for if in the slightest degree tainted or musty, it infallibly communicates a very disagreeable taste to the broth; besides, fresh meat gives a more savoury broth than meat that has been kept for two or three days. It is also advisable to score the meat and to cut it into slices, or to bruise it with a mallet or cleaver.

Two pounds of muscular beef scored and cut into slices, affords a stronger and far more savoury broth, than 3 lbs. of the same beef when boiled in one piece. Cooks usually allow for good broth, one pound of muscular meat, to two quarts of water, and they suffer the fluid to simmer till reduced, by evaporation, to one pint, or one pint and a half. A second decoction may be made by again covering the meat with a less quantity of water, and suffering it to boil, taking care to supply the water from time to time as it becomes evaporated.

This reminds us of Rabelais, the humorous vicar of Meudon, who distinguishes, in his jocose way, two sorts of broths. (*Bouillon de Prime,*) prime-broth; and broth good for hounds; (*Bouillon de levriers,*) the meaning of which stands as follows.[25] The first designates that premature delibation of broth which the young monks in the convent used to steal, when they could, from the kitchen, in their way to the choir at the hour of "*Prime,*" a service which was performed at about seven or eight in the morning, when the porridge-pot, with all its ingredients, had been boiling for the space of one or two hours, and when the broth, full of eyes swimming gently on the golden surface, had already obtained an interesting appearance and taste. On the contrary, greyhound's broth, (*Bouillon de levriers,*) means that portion of the porridge which was served to the novices after an ample *presumption* in favour of the *Magnates* of the monastery. This was good for nothing, and monks of inferior ranks were ready to throw it to the dogs.

[25] Tabella Cibaria, p. 23.

The flavouring ingredients, which are usually the domestic pot-herbs and indigenous roots, such as cellery, carrots, &c. should be added at the end of the process, to prevent their aromatic substances becoming dissipated by long simmering.

Dr. Kitchener[26] says, "meat from which broth has been made, is excellently well prepared for *potting*, and is quite as good, or better than that which has been boiled, till it is dry."

[26] The Cook's Oracle, p. 103.

SOUP.

Soups are decoctions of meat which differ from broth, in being more concentrated, and usually also more complex in their composition. They are in fact strong broths, containing either farinaceous roots and seeds, or other parts of vegetable substances.

The erudite editor of the *"Almanach des Gourmands"*[27] tells us, that ten folio volumes would not contain the receipts of all the soups that have been invented in that grand school of good eating, the Parisian kitchen. The author of *Apicius Redivivus*[28] says "the general fault of our English soups seems to be the employment of an excess of spice, and too small a portion of roots and herbs." "*Point des Legumes, point de Cuisiniere,*" is deservedly the common adage of the French kitchen. A better soup may be made with a couple of pounds of meat, and plenty of vegetables, than our common cooks will make with four times that quantity of meat. The great art of composing a rich soup consists in so proportioning the several flavouring ingredients, that no particular taste predominates."—One pound and a half of meat at least ought to be allowed for making a quart of soup. The full flavour can only be obtained by long and slow simmering the meat, during which time the vessel should be kept covered to prevent the evaporation of the fluid as much as possible.

[27] Vol. II. page 30.
[28] Or the Cook's Oracle, 2d edit. Vol. 97.

The flavouring ingredients should not be added till ten or fifteen minutes before the soup is finished. Clear soups should be perfectly transparent, and thickened soups, should be of the consistence of cream.

The soup, says a writer, on Cookery, might be called the portal of the edifice of a French dinner, either plain or sumptuous. It is a *sine qua non* article. It leads to the several courses constituting the essence of the repast, and lays the unsophisticated foundation upon which the whole is to rest, as upon a solid basis, in the stomach. It is, perhaps, the most wholesome food that can be used; and the gaunt, yet strong frame of the French soldiery, has long experienced the benefit of it. They vulgarly say, "*C'est la soupe qui fait le Soldat.*" 'It is the soup that makes the soldier.' Partial to this mess, they have it daily in barracks, in their marches, and in the camp; and they often swallow a large bowl of broth and bread, in the morning a few minutes before the trumpets calls them to the field of battle.

PIES

Are those dishes which consist either of meat, or of fruit, covered with a farinaceous crust, enriched with butter or other fat, and rendered fit for eating by baking.

The crust of the pie is usually made of two parts by weight of wheaten flour, and one part of butter, lard, or other fat.

The flour is made into a stiff paste with cold water, and rolled out on a board with a paste pin to the thickness of about one quarter of an inch, the board being previously sprinkled over with flour to prevent the dough from sticking to the board. About one-sixth part of the butter, in pieces of the size of a nutmeg, is put over the extended paste, and the whole again dusted with flour; the paste is then doubled up and rolled out as before. A like portion of butter is again distributed over the paste, which, after being doubled up, is rolled out, and the same operation is repeated till the whole quantity of butter is thus incorporated with the flour.

Part of the paste is then laid, one quarter or half an inch in thickness, over the inside of a deep dish in which the pie is to be baked, and the meat, cut in chops or slices, is put into the dish, together with the seasonings, and a portion of water or gravy, about one tea cup full, to one pound of meat. The contents of the basin are then covered with a lid, made of the remainder of the paste, rolled out rather thicker than the inside lining of the dish, and the lid is made to adhere to the inside sheeting, which should extend over the rim of the dish, by pressing the top paste close upon the margin. A few small holes are then made in the top crust, and the pie is put in the oven.

The baking should be slow. If the pie be put into a hot oven, the crust becomes hard, and many a cook is blamed for making bad pies, when the fault really lies with the baker. A light and flaky pie crust can only be produced by the judicious application in the manner stated, of the butter, or fatty matter. By this means the butter is distributed, in distinct layers, through the mass of the pie crust. The flour dusted over each layer prevents the paste forming one mass, or, as it is called, becoming heavy. The more frequently, therefore, the paste is rolled out with butter, lard, or other fat, interposed between each layer, provided the layers are dusted over with flour, the more flaky will be the pie; and hence, also, by increasing the quantity of butter, to a certain limit, the flakeness of the pie crust becomes increased.

Pastry cooks usually allow from ten to twelve ounces of butter to one pound of flour for making a light puff paste, such as they use for tarts and patties.

PUDDINGS

Are of two kinds; the first consists of a farinaceous dough, containing a portion of butter or other fat, inclosing any kind of meat or fruit, and rendered eatable by boiling; it may be termed *a boiled pie.*

The paste for a meat pudding is usually made with beef suet, or marrow, one part of it chopped as fine as possible, and intimately mixed with four parts by weight of flour, is made into a paste with water or milk. With this paste, a pudding mould or basin, previously rubbed with butter within, is lined, and the meat is added to fill up the vacancy. A lid of paste is now put over the meat, and made to adhere to the margin of the dish. The whole is then tied over with a wetted cloth, dusted with flour to prevent the dough sticking to it, and then boiled in water till the pudding is sufficiently cooked.

The other kind of pudding is a batter composed of eggs, butter and flour, or any other farinaceous substance, occasionally enriched with the admixture of fruit, sugar, and spices, and rendered eatable either by boiling in the manner stated, or by baking in an oven.

MADE DISHES,

So called to distinguish them from plain, roasted, boiled, or fried meat; are usually composed of flesh, fish, poultry, or vegetables, stewed with gravy, butter, cream, or other savoury sauces. The composition of made dishes is generally from printed or written receipts, except when done by what are termed professed cooks, who, understanding completely their business, follow their own judgment, in aid of the receipt. There is a mistake very common in supposing that there is a great difficulty in cooking such dishes, though there is indeed much trouble; but if a mistake is made, it can in general be remedied, which is not the case in the mere simple operations of roasting and boiling, where a mistake is very often irreparable.

When we take a view of the chemical composition of made dishes, we soon perceive that they are all compounds of animal and vegetable substances, rendered sapid or agreeable to the palate by strong decoctions of meat, gravy, and spices, of various descriptions; all of them abound in animal gelatine and vegetable mucilage, or farinaceous matter, rendered soluble in water. The quantity of spices is generally small, "[29]their presence should be rather supposed than perceived, they are the invisible spirit of good cookery."

[29] Dr. Kitchiner's Cook's Oracle, p. 493.

OBSERVATIONS ON MADE DISHES.

Made dishes are sometimes very expensive, and sometimes very economical, for ragouts and fricassees are often much less expensive than the plain dishes made of the same material, that is, a given weight of meat will go farther than if plainly roasted or boiled. French cookery consists nearly altogether of made dishes, both with the rich and poor. The rich have them to gratify the palate, and the poor, for the sake of economy. Many circumstances combine to prevent made dishes from becoming of very general or frequent use in England. The care, attention, and length of time necessary for preparing them, are incompatible with the domestic affairs and usages of life in this country, where time is far more precious than in any other country; it is for that reason, most probably, that all the operations of English cookery are such as can be performed expeditiously.

The English cooks, both in the middling and lower ranks, are generally in a hurry to get a dinner dressed. The French cooks, on the contrary, begin in the morning early, and even in the house of the simple *Bourgois*, the dinner begins to be cooked immediately after breakfast.

The superior expedition, and inferior degree of skill which distinguish English from French cookery, would be sufficient alone to give the former the preference in this country; but there are a number of other circumstances that have the same tendency.

A good table is a study in France: it is with the master a grand object in life, and with the cooks a constant employment, like our journeymen in a manufactory. With us, again, the dinner is readily prepared, and expeditiously eaten. It is despatched like a piece of business in this country; but in France, and more or less all over the Continent, people dine as if they had a pleasure in dining; they converse more during the repast than almost at any other time, and they never hurry it over as if they were in haste to be done, and as if they had business always on their mind, and were reflecting on the saying, so common and so true, that "*time is money.*"

It is curious enough, however, to remark, that the French, who sit so long, and enjoy themselves so leisurely at dinner, rise, immediately after the dessert, from the table, and are ready for business; and that the English, who hurry the dinner over, pass whole hours over the bottle as if time were of no value. Such are the inconsistencies of mankind, arising from different tastes and different circumstances.

The construction of our kitchen grates and fire places, and the nature of the fuel we burn, are unfavourable to the slow and regular simmering with which made dishes are prepared; and, at the same time, that they are unfavourable for made dishes, they are exactly what is wanted for English cookery. The construction of the grates, together with the nature of the fuel, produce a fierce scorching fire, so that the direct rays of heat may be made to impinge on the substance to be cooked.

In France, roasting large joints is almost impracticable with the form and nature of the fire; so that it does not appear that taste or will has been the only guide in the mode of cooking in either country; but that the practices most suitable to circumstances have been a chief cause of the great difference of the manner of dressing victuals.

English medical men have always been at great pains to condemn made dishes as injurious to health; but the French physicians have been of a different opinion, and if *experientia docet* is a true proverb, they ought to be the best judges: but those who have been used to both, will allow that they are less heavy, and the stomach seems to be less encumbered after the French dinner on made dishes, than the English one on single joints.

In made dishes, where butcher's meat enters, as although the chief ingredient is generally *much more* done, to use the common phrase, none of its nutritive substances are lost; but as the arguments for and against the real things of one or the other is not to be determined by reason, and has not been determined by experience, it would be absurd to give an opinion on the subject.

It may be well enough, however, to observe, that the dispute about what are the most healthy dishes, probably arises from difference of tastes, and from those things to which the stomach has not been accustomed, not agreeing with it at first; so that most people on finding it so, if they can avoid doing it, never repeat the experiment.

The case is the same with Foreigners as with Englishmen, for their stomachs do not at first find our dishes agree with them.

GRAVY.

When the muscular part of meat is gradually exposed to a very moderate heat, sufficient to brown the outer fibres, the gelatine, osmazome, and other animal juices of it, become disengaged, and separated in a liquid state, and constitute a fluid of a brown colour, possessing a highly savoury and grateful taste. Hence gravy is the soluble constituent or liquid part of meat, which, spontaneously, exudes from flesh, when gradually exposed to a continued heat sufficient to corrugate the animal fibre. Flavouring vegetables are often added, and fried with the meat, such as sliced onions, carrots or cellery, till they are tender, together with some spices and the usual condiments.

To extract gravy, the meat is cut into thin slices, or it is scored, and the fibres are bruised with a mallet. It is then usually seasoned, with pepper and salt, and exposed in a pan containing a small quantity of butter, or other fat, (or without any fat,) to the action of a gradual heat, just sufficient to brown the outer fibre strongly. The juices of the meat, which are thus during the frying process, copiously disengaged, are suffered to remain exposed to the action of heat till they have assumed the consistence of a thin cream, and a brown colour. A small portion of water is then added to re-dissolve the extracted mass, and after the whole has been suffered to simmer with the spices and roots for a short time, together with an additional quantity of water, the liquid is strained off through a sieve. If the gravy be intended for made dishes, it is customary to give it the consistence of cream, by means of *thickening paste*. (See p. 160.) The meat is capable of furnishing an additional quantity of gravy. It is therefore covered with water and suffered to simmer for about one hour, or till the fluid is reduced to one half its bulk.

One pound and a quarter of lean beef, or one pound and a half of veal, will afford one pint of strong gravy.

When broth, soups, or gravy, are preserved from day to day, in hot weather, they should be warmed up every day, and put into fresh scalded pans, this renders them less liable to spoil.

SAUCES.

"The fundamental principle of all,
Is what ingenious cooks, the *relish* call;
For when the markets send in loads of food,
They all are tasteless till that makes them good."

Dr. King's Art of Cookery.

Sauces are intended to heighten the taste and give a savoury flavour to a dish, flesh, fish, fowl, or vegetables.

In England there is little variety in those kind of relishes, and it was observed by a foreigner, with a good deal of wit, and a great deal of truth, "that the English had a great variety of forms of religion and no variety in their sauces; whereas, in France they had uniformity in the former, and an infinite variety in the latter."

Melted butter is the grand and chief basis of most English sauces. Melted butter and oysters, melted butter and parsley, melted butter and anchovies, melted butter and eggs, melted butter and shrimps, melted butter and lobsters, melted butter and capers, are nearly all the sauces used in England. Besides these, the following flavouring substances are in common use: *viz.* mushrooms, onions, spices, sweet herbs, wine, soy, and the usual condiments, but melted butter, gravy, or some farinaceous mucilage, form the basis of all sauces. These substances combined in different proportions are quite sufficient to make an endless variety of picquant sauces, as pleasant to the palate and stomach, as the most compound foreign sauces in which every thing has the same taste, and none its own taste. The aim of the English cooks, as far as it regards sauces, appears to be to let every sauce display a decided character, so as to taste only of the material from which it derives its name. *Compound sauces* are seldom employed, but in the *learned* foreign dishes.

What has been observed, relative to time used in the article, of *made dishes*, namely, that it was in this country too valuable to be bestowed on eating, or on preparing to eat, applies also in the case of making sauces.

Nothing can be made more easily than the English sauces, but the variety of French sauces are great, and much skill and time are necessary for preparing most of them.

THICKENING PASTE FOR BROTH, SOUP, GRAVY, AND MADE DISHES.

It is customary to thicken some dishes with a compound of two parts of flour and one of butter, first made into a paste by heating slowly the ingredients in a pan, till the mass acquires a yellow gold colour, the flour and butter being stirred all the time to prevent the mass from burning to the bottom of the pan. The substance thus obtained is called *thickening*, or *thickening paste*, for it is the basis employed by cooks for thickening soups, gravies, stews, sauces, and other dishes. The mass readily combines with water; a large table spoonful is sufficient to thicken a quart of meat broth. Besides this *thickening paste*, other farinaceous substances are employed for that purpose, such as bread raspings, crumbs of stale bread, biscuit powder, potatoe mucilage, oatmeal, sago powder, rice powder, &c. A cow-heel, on account of the vast quantity of gelatine with which it abounds, is excellently well calculated for giving *body* to soups: the cow-heel, after being cracked, is boiled with the broth or soup.

COLOURING FOR BROTH, SOUP, GRAVIES, AND MADE DISHES.

The substance employed for colouring soups, gravies, broths, and other dishes, requiring a brown colour, is burnt sugar. This imparts to the dish a fine yellowish brown tinge, without giving any sensible flavour to the dish. Eight ounces of powdered lump sugar, and two or three table spoonfuls of water, are suffered to boil gently in an iron pan, till the mass has assumed a dark brown colour, which takes place when all the water is evaporated, and the sugar begins to be partly charred by the action of the heat. The mass is then removed from the fire, and about a quarter of a pint of water is gradually added to effect a solution. The fluid thus obtained is of a syrupy consistence, and of a fine dark brown colour; a small quantity gives to broth, soup, or gravy, a bright orange colour, without altering sensibly the flavour of the dish. Some cooks add to it mushroom catsup and port wine.

STOCK FOR MAKING EXTEMPORANEOUS BROTH, SOUP, OR GRAVY.

The name of *stock* is given to meat jelly produced from a decoction of meat, so highly concentrated that the fluid, when cold, exhibits an elastic tremulous consistence.

The meat is slowly boiled in water, with the customary seasonings, as pot herbs, or esculent roots, and the decoction skimmed, and continued to simmer till it is charged with a sufficient quantity of animal matter to form a jelly when cold; this degree of concentration is known by removing, from time to time, a portion of the fluid, and suffering it to cool. When the decoction has been so far concentrated, it is strained off through a sieve and suffered to repose, that the insoluble part, if any, may subside. When this has been effected, the clear fluid is suffered to cool, which causes the fatty matter it contains to become collected at the surface, where it forms a cake or crust, which is to be removed. The substance underneath is a tremulous jelly; it is called first stock, or long broth, (*Le grand bouillon* of the French kitchen). If the jelly be not transparent it is re-melted by a gentle heat, and clarified by the addition of the white of eggs added to it, as soon as it is liquified. This substance becoming coagulated at the boiling heat, entangles with it the parts mechanically diffused through the jelly, and rises to the top as a dense scum. It may then be removed by a skimmer. The name of *second-stock* (*Jus de bœuf* of the French) is given to a more concentrate jelly of meat made in a similar manner. It is chiefly employed as the basis of all savoury made dishes and rich sauces, whilst the former serves for making extemporaneous soups. *Second stock* is usually prepared in the following manner:—Put into a stew-pan about half a pound of lean bacon or ham, a few carrots and onions, two or three cloves, about six or eight pounds of lean beef, and a shin of beef of about the same weight, break the bone, and having scored the meat, suffer it to simmer over a very gentle fire, with about two quarts of *first stock*, or better put it into an oven, and suffer it to stew, till the liquid assumes a light brown colour. When this has taken place, add to the mass six quarts of boiling water, suffer it to boil up gently, and remove the scum as it rises; and suffer it to evaporate till reduced to about three quarts, then strain it through a sieve, and clarify it as before directed.

OBSERVATIONS ON THE CHOICE OF MEAT.

The flesh of animals which are suddenly killed when in high health, so far as the palate is concerned, is not yet fit for the table, although fully nutritious and in perfection for making soup; because sometime after the death, the muscular parts suffer contraction—their fibres become rigid. When this has taken place, the flesh is not long in experiencing the commencement of those chemical changes which terminate in putrefaction; and it is of the utmost importance, in domestic economy, to take care that all large joints of meat be in this intermediate state when they are cooked: for no skill in the culinary art will compensate for negligence in this point, as every one must have often experienced to his great disappointment.

The degree of inteneration may be known by the flesh yielding readily to the pressure of the finger, and by its opposing little resistance to an attempt to bend the joint. Poultry also thus part readily with their feathers; and it would be advisable to leave a few when the bird is plucked, in order to assist in determining their state.

The following wholesome advice on this subject we copy from Doctor Kitchiner:[30]—"*When you order meat, poultry, or fish, tell the tradesman when you intend to dress it,* and he will then have it in his power to serve you with provision that will do him credit, which the finest meat, &c. in the world, will never do, unless it has been kept a proper time to be ripe and tender. If you have a well-ventilated larder, in a shady, dry situation, you may make still surer, by ordering in your meat and poultry, such a time before you want it as will render it tender, which the finest meat cannot be, unless hung a proper time, according to the season and nature of the meat, &c. but always till it has made some very slight advance towards putrefaction."

[30] The Cook's Oracle.

Ox-beef
—when of a young animal, has a shining oily smoothness, a fine open grain, and dark florid red colour. The fat is splendish yellowish white. If the animal has been fed upon oil cakes, the fat has a golden yellow colour.

Cow-Beef

—is closer in the grain than ox-beef, but the muscular parts are not of so bright a red colour. In old meat there is a streak of cartilage or bone in the ribs, called by butchers, *the crush-bone*; the harder this is, the older has been the animal.

Veal.
—The flesh of a bull calf is firmer, but not in general so white as that of a cow calf. Exposures to the air for some time reddens the colour of the flesh. Veal is best of which the kidney is well covered with thick white hard fat.

Mutton.
—A *wether*, five years old, affords the most delicate meat. The grain of the meat should be fine, and the fat white and firm. The leg of a *wether mutton* is known by a round lump of fat on the insides of the thigh, the leg of an *ewe* by the udder.

Lamb.
—The flesh of fine lamb looks of a delicate pale red colour; the fat is splendid white, but it does not possess a great solidity. *Grass Lamb* is in season from Easter to Michaelmas. *House Lamb* from Christmas to Lady-day.

Pork.
—This species of meat of the best fed animals is particularly fine grained, and may be bruised by forcibly pressing it between the fingers. The skin of the young animal is thin; the flesh of old pigs is hard and tough, and the skin very thick. The prime season for pork is from Michaelmas to March. The western pigs, chiefly those of Berks, Oxford, and Bucks, possess a decided superiority over the eastern of Essex, Suffolk, and Norfolk.

Hare.
—To ascertain its age, examine the first joint of the fore foot; you will find a small knob, if it is a *leveret*, which disappears as the hare grows older; then examine the ears; if they tear easily, the animal is young. When newly killed, the body is stiff; as it grows stale, it becomes flaccid.

Venison
—is of a darker colour than mutton. If the fat be clear, bright and thick, and the cleft of the hoof smooth and close, it is young, but if the cleft is wide and tough, it is old. By pushing a skewer or knife under the bone which sticks out of a haunch or shoulder, the odour of the skewer will tell whether the meat be fresh or tainted. Venison is best flavoured in the month of August, the animal should not be killed till he is about four years old.

Fowls
—for boiling should be chosen as white as possible, those which have black legs had better be roasted. The season of perfection in poultry is just before they have quite come to their full growth. Chickens three months old are very delicate. Age makes a striking difference in the flesh of fowls, since after the age of twelve months it becomes tougher. The cock indeed, at that age, is only used for making soup.

Pigeons
—are in their greatest perfection in September, there is then the most plentiful and best food for them; their finest growth is just when they are full feathered. When they are in the pen-feathers, they are flabby; when they are full grown, and have flown some time, they are hard.

Pheasants
—may be distinguished by the *length* and *sharpness* of their *spurs*, which in the younger ones are *short* and *blunt*.

Partridges
—if old are always to be known during the early part of the season, by their legs being of a pale blue, instead of a yellowish brown colour: "so that when a Londoner receives his brace of blue legged birds in September, he should immediately snap their legs and draw out the sinews, by means of pulling off the feet, instead of leaving them to torment him, like so many strings, when he would be wishing to enjoy his repast." This remedy to make the legs tender, removes the objection to old birds, provided the weather will admit of their being sufficiently long kept. If birds are overkept, their eyes will be much sunk, and the trail becomes soft, and somewhat discoloured. The first place to ascertain if they are beginning to be tainted, is the inside of the bill.

Fish, and *Crimping of Fish*.
—Both sea and river fish cannot be eaten too fresh. The gills should be of a fine red colour, the eyes glistening, the scales brilliant, and the whole fish should feel stiff and firm, if soft or flabby the fish is old.

To improve the quality of fish, they are sometimes subject to the process called *crimping*. The operation has been examined by Mr. Carlisle, to whom we are indebted for the following particulars:

"Whenever the rigid contractions of death have not taken place, this process may be practised with success. The sea fish destined for crimping, are usually struck on the head when caught, which it is said protracts the term of the contractibility and the muscles which retain the property longest are those about the head. Many transverse sections of the muscles being made, and the fish immersed in cold water, the contractions called crimping takes place in about five minutes, but if the mass be large, it often requires 30 minutes to complete the process. The crimping of fresh water fish is said to require hard water, and the London fishmongers usually employ it."

Mr. Carlisle found, that by crimping, the muscles subjected to the process have both their absolute weight, and their specific gravity increased, so that it appears, that water is absorbed and condensation takes place. It was also observed that the effect was greater in proportion to the vivaciousness of the fish.

From these observations, it appears, that the object of crimping is first to retard the natural stiffening of the muscles, and then by the sudden application of cold water, to excite it in the greatest possible degree, by which means the flesh both acquires the desired firmness and keeps longer.

ON KEEPING OF MEAT, AND BEST CONSTRUCTION OF LARDERS, PANTRIES AND MEAT SAFES.

Larders, pantries and safes, for keeping meat, should be sheltered from the direct rays of the sun, and otherwise guarded against the influence of warmth. All places where provisions are kept should be so constructed that a brisk current of cool air can be made to pass through them at command. With this view it would be advisable to have openings on all sides of larders, or meat safes, which might be closed or opened according to the way from which the wind blows, the time of the day, or season of the year; they should be kept, too, with the greatest attention to cleanliness. It will be better also if the sides or walls of meat safes are occasionally scoured with soap, or soap and slacked quicklime.

Warm weather is the worst for keeping meat; the south wind has long been noted as being hostile to keeping provisions. Juvenal, in his 4th Satire, says:

> "Now sickly autumn to dry frost give way,
> Cold winter rag'd and fresh preserved the prey;
> Yet with such haste the busy fisher flew,
> As if hot south-wind corruption blew."

A joint of meat may be preserved for several days in the midst of summer by wrapping it in a clean linen cloth, previously moistened with strong vinegar, and sprinkled over with salt, and then placing it in an earthenware pan, or hanging it up, and changing the cloth, or ringing it out a-fresh, and again steeping it in vinegar once a day, if the weather be very hot.

The best meat for keeping is *mutton*, and the leg keeps best, and may with care, if the temperature be only moderate, be preserved without becoming tainted for about a week; during frost a leg of mutton will keep a fortnight.

A shoulder of *mutton* is next to the leg the joint best calculated for keeping in warm weather.

The scrag end of a neck is very liable to become tainted; it cannot be kept with safety during hot weather for more than two days.

The kernels, or glands, in the thick part of the leg should be dissected out, because the mucous matter in which they abound speedily becomes putrid, and then tends very much to infect the adjoining part.

The chine and rib-bones should be wiped, and sprinkled over with salt and pepper, and the bloody part of the neck should be removed. In the brisket, the commencement of the putrefactive process takes place in the breast, and if this part is to be kept, it is advisable to guard against it becoming tainted, by sprinkling a little salt and pepper over it: the vein, or pipe near the bone of the inside of a chine of mutton should be cut out, and if the meat is to be kept for some time, the part close round the tail should be sprinkled with salt, after having first cut out the gland or kernel.

In *beef* the ribs are less liable to become tainted than any other joint; they may be kept in a cool pantry in the summer months for six days, and ten days in winter.

The round of beef will not keep long, unless sprinkled over with salt. All the glands or kernels which it contains should be dissected out.

The brisket is still more liable to become tainted by keeping, it cannot be kept sweet with safety more than three days in summer, and about a week in winter.

Lamb is the next in order for keeping, though it is considered best to eat it soon, or even the day after it is killed. If it is not very young the leg will keep four or five days, with care, in a cool place in summer.

Veal and *Pork*—a leg will keep very well in summer for three or four days, and a week in winter:—but the scrag end of veal or pork will not keep well above a day in summer, and two or three days in winter.

The part that becomes tainted first of a leg of veal is where the udder is skewered back. The skewer should be taken out, and both that and the part beneath it wiped dry every day, by which means it will keep good three or four days in warm weather. The vein or *pipe* that runs along the chine of a loin of veal should be cut out, as is usually done in mutton and beef. The skirt of a breast of veal should likewise be taken off, and the inside of the breast wiped, scraped, and sprinkled with salt.

PRESERVATION OF ANIMAL SUBSTANCES IN A RECENT STATE.

As the supply of food is always subject to irregularities, the preservation of the excess, obtained at one time, to meet the deficiency of another, would soon engage the attention of mankind. At first this method would be simple and natural, and derived from a very limited observation, but in the progress of society, the wants and occupations of mankind would lead them to invent means, by which the more perishable alimentary substances of one season, might be reserved for the consumption of another, or the superfluous productions of distant countries might be transported to others where they are more needed.

PICKLING AND DRY SALTING OF MEAT.

Common salt is advantageously employed as an antiseptic, to preserve aliments from spontaneous decomposition, and particularly to prevent the putrefaction of animal food. In general, however, the large quantity of salt which is necessarily employed in this way, deteriorates the alimentary properties of the meat, and the longer it has been preserved, the less wholesome and digestible does it become.

Meat, however, which has not been too long preserved, simply pickled, or *corned* meat as it is called, is but little injured or decomposed, it is still succulent and tender, easily digested, nourishing and wholesome enough.

The property of salt to preserve animal substances from putrefaction is of the most essential importance to the empire in general, and to the remote grazing districts in particular. It enables the latter to dispose of their live stock, and distant navigation is wholly dependant upon it. All kinds of animal substances may be preserved by salt, but beef and pork are the only staple articles of this kind. In general, the pieces of the animal best fitted for being salted are those which contain fewest large blood vessels, and are most solid. Some recommend all the glands to be cut out, they say, that without this precaution meat cannot be preserved; but this is a mistake, a dry salter of eminence, informs me, that it is not essential, provided the glands or kernels are properly covered with salt.

The salting may be performed either by dry rubbing, or better by immersing the meat in a salt pickle. Cured in the former way the meat will keep longer, but it is more altered in its valuable properties; in the latter way it is more delicate and nutritious. Eight pounds of salt, one pound of sugar, and four ounces of saltpetre, boiled for a few minutes with four gallons of water, skimmed and allowed to cool, forms a strong pickle, which will preserve meat completely immersed in it. To effect this, which is essential, either a heavy board, or flat stone, must be laid upon the meat. The same pickle may be used repeatedly, provided it be boiled up occasionally with additional salt to restore its strength, diminished by the combination of part of the salt with the meat, and by the dilution of the pickle by the juices of the meat extracted. By boiling, the albumen, which would cause the pickle to spoil, is coagulated, and rises in the form of scum, which must be carefully removed.

Beef and pork, although properly salted with salt alone, acquire a green colour; but if an ounce of saltpetre be added to each five pounds of salt employed, the muscular fibre acquires a fine red tinge; but this improvement in appearance is more than compensated by its becoming harder and harsher to the taste; to correct which, a proportion of sugar or molasses is often added. But the red colour may be given if desired, without hardening the meat, by the addition of a little cochineal.

Meat kept immersed in pickle rather gains weight. In one experiment by Messrs. Donkin and Gamble, there was a gain of three per cent. and in another of two and a half; but in the common way of salting, when the meat is not immersed in pickle there is a loss of about one pound, or one and a half in sixteen.

Dry salting is performed by rubbing the surface of the meat all over with salt; and it is generally believed that the process of salting is promoted if the salt be rubbed in with a heavy hand. However this may be, it is almost certain that very little salt penetrates, except through the cut surfaces, to which it should therefore be chiefly applied; and all holes, whether natural or artificial, should be particularly attended to. For each twenty-five pounds of meat, about two pounds of coarse grained salt should be allowed, and the whole, previously heated, rubbed in at once. When laid in the pickling tub, a brine is soon formed by the salt dissolved in the juice of the meat which it extracts, and with this the meat should be wetted every day, and a different side turned down. In ten or twelve days it will be sufficiently cured.

For domestic use the meat should not be salted as soon as it comes from the market, but kept until its fibre has become short and tender, as these changes do not take place after it has been acted upon by the salt. But in the provision trade, "the expedition with which the animals are slaughtered, the meat cut up and salted, and afterwards packed, is astonishing."[31]

[31] Wakefield's Ireland, vol. I. p. 750.

By salting the meat while still warm, and before the fluids are coagulated, the salt penetrates immediately, by means of the vessels, through the whole substance of the meat; and hence meat is admirably cured at Tunis, even in the hottest season, so that Mr. Jackson, in his *Reflections on the Trade in the Mediterranean*, recommends ships being supplied there with their provisions.

The following mixture of condiments is exceedingly well calculated for dry salting.

Take a pound of black pepper, a quarter of a pound of Cayenne pepper, and a pound of saltpetre, all ground very fine; mix these three well together, and blend them alternately with about three *quarts* of very fine salt: this mixture is sufficient for eight hundred weight of beef. As the pieces are brought from the person cutting up, first sprinkle the pieces with the spice, and introduce a little into all the thickest parts; if it cannot be done otherwise, make a small incision with a knife. The first salter, after rubbing salt and spice well into the meat, should take and mould the piece, the same as washing a shirt upon a board; this may be very easily done, and the meat being lately killed, is soft and pliable; this moulding opens the grain of the meat, which will make it imbibe the spice and salt much quicker than the common method of salting. The first salter hands his piece over to the second salter, who moulds and rubs the salt well into the meat, and if he observes occasion, introduces the spice; when the second salter has finished his piece, he folds it up as close as possible, and hands it to the packer at the *harness* or salting tubs, who must be stationed near him: the packer must be careful to pack his *harness* tubs as close as possible.

All the work must be carried on in the shade, but where there is a strong current of air, the *harness* tubs in particular; this being a very material point in curing the meat in a hot climate. Meat may be cured in this manner with the greatest safety, when the thermometer, in the shade, is at 110°, the extreme heat assisting the curing.

A good sized bullock, of six or seven hundred weight, may be killed and salted within the hour.

The person who attends with the spice near the first salter, has the greatest trust imposed upon him; besides the spice, he should be well satisfied that the piece is sufficiently salted, before he permits the first salter to hand the piece over to the second salter.

All the salt should be very fine, and the packer, besides sprinkling the bottom of his *harness* tubs, should be careful to put plenty of salt between each tier of meat, which is very soon turned into the finest pickle. The pickle will nearly cover the meat, as fast as the packer can stow it away. It is always a good sign that the meat is very safe when the packer begins to complain that his hands are aching with cold.

By this method there is no doubt but that the meat is perfectly cured in three hours from the time of killing the bullock: the saltpetre in a very little time strikes through the meat; however, it is always better to let it lie in the *harness* tubs till the following morning, when it will have an exceeding pleasant smell on opening the *harness* tubs; then take it out and pack it in tight barrels, with its own pickle.

METHOD OF PREPARING BACON, HAMS, AND HUNG BEEF.

Meat, when salted, is sometimes dried, when it gets the name of bacon, ham, or hung beef.

The drying of salt meat is effected either by hanging it in a dry and well-aired place, or by exposing it at the same time to wood smoke, which gives it a peculiar flavour, much admired in Westphalia hams and Hamburgh beef, and also tends to preserve it, by the antiseptic action of the pyrolignic acid. When meat is to be hung, it need not be so highly salted.

The method of preparing bacon is peculiar to certain districts. The following is the method of making bacon in Hampshire and Somersetshire:—

The season for killing hogs for bacon is between October and March. The articles to be salted are sprinkled over with bay-salt, and put for twenty-four hours in the salting trough, to allow the adhering blood to drain away. After this they take them out, wipe them very dry, and throw away the draining. They then take some fresh bay-salt, and heating it well in a frying-pan, rub the meat very well with it, repeating this every day for four days, turning the sides every other day.

If the hog be very large, they keep the sides in brine, turning them occasionally for three weeks; after which they take them out, and let them be thoroughly dried in the usual manner.

SMOKE-DRYING, OR CURING OF BACON, HAMS, AND BEEF, AS PRACTISED IN WESTPHALIA.

The custom of fumigating hams with wood smoke is of a very ancient date, it was well known to the Romans, and Horace mentions it.[32]

"*Fumosæ cum pede pernæ.*"

[32] Sat. II. 2-117.

Several places on the Continent are famous for the delicacy and flavour of their hams; Westphalia, however, is at the head of the list.

The method of curing bacon and hams in Westphalia (in Germany) is as follows: Families that kill one or more hogs a year, which is a common practice in private houses, have a closet in the garret, joining to the chimney, made tight, to retain smoke, in which they hang their hams and bacon to dry; and out of the effect of the fire, that they may be gradually dried by the wood smoke, and not by heat.

The smoke of the fuel is conveyed into the closet by a hole in the chimney, near the floor, and a place is made for an iron stopper to be thrust into the funnel of the chimney, to force the smoke through the hole into the closet. The smoke is carried off again by another hole in the funnel of the chimney, above the said stopper, almost at the ceiling, where it escapes. The upper hole must not be too big, because the closet must be always full of smoke, and that from wood fires. Or the bacon and hams are simply placed in the vicinity of an open fire-place, where wood is burned, so as to be exposed to the smoke of the wood.

METHOD OF CURING HAMS, BEEF, AND FISH, BY MEANS OF PYRO-LIGNEOUS ACID.

The following account of the preservative quality of pyro-ligneous[33] acid, exhibited in a memoir by Dr. Wilkinson to the Bath Society, is highly important:—

[33] Philosophical Magazine, 1821, No. 273, p. 12.

"Mr. Sockett having directed his attention to the smoking of hams with wood smoke, either in a building erected for that purpose, or in a chimney where wood alone is burned, in addition to its considerable increase of flavour, he considered it more effectually preserved from putrefaction by being, what is commonly called, smoke-dried. Mr. Sockett having ascertained by experiments, that meat thus cured required less salt, he was induced to suppose some antiseptic quality in the same, and not attributable to the mere application of heat. A neighbouring manufactory of pyro-ligneous acid afforded him an opportunity of trying a variety of experiments, which convinced him of the correctness of the supposition of the antiseptic quality of wood smoke, as the same effects as to flavour and preservation were produced in a superior degree without the aid of any increase of temperature, which, by drying, diminishes the nutritious quality of meat thus exposed."

"Mr. Sockett ascertained, that if a ham had the reduced quantity of salt usually employed for smoke-dried hams, and was then exposed to smoke, putrefaction soon took place when pyro-ligneous acid was not used; even one half this reduced portion of salt is sufficient when it is used, being applied cold, and the ham is thus effectually cured without any loss of weight, and retaining more animal juices."

"The mode adopted was by adding about two table-spoonfuls of pyro-ligneous acid to the pickle for a ham of 10 or 12 lbs.; and when taken out of the pickle, previous to being hung up, painted over with the acid, by means of a brush. In many instances, Mr. Sockett has succeeded by brushing the ham over with the acid, without adding any to the pickle. The same mode answers equally well with tongues, requiring a little more acid, on account of the thickness and hardness of the integuments."

"Upon dried salmon it answers admirably; brushing it over once or twice had a better effect than two months smoking in the usual way, and without the same loss from rancidity. From the result of a few experiments on herrings, he is persuaded that this mode of curing might be most advantageously introduced in our fisheries, so that herrings might be cured here superior to those imported from Holland."

"These experiments so satisfactorily demonstrating the antiseptic qualities of this acid, where only small portions of salt were employed, Mr. Sockett was then induced to try the results of the application of this acid when no salt was employed: he placed some beef steaks upon a plate, and covered the bottom with the acid, the steaks being daily turned; and at the time of recording the experiment, he noticed that they kept above six weeks without the least tendency to putrefaction: this experiment was made in the middle of July 1815."

"Not only Mr. Sockett, but many families in Swansea, and its vicinity, practise, with the greatest success, this mode of curing hams, tongues, beef, fish, &c."

"This acid is very easily and cheaply prepared: the first distilled product of the wood, in that state denominated black acid, answers the best when separated from its tar and naphtha. More than 70 gallons of acid, sufficiently strong, are procured from a ton of wood; a gallon is quite sufficient for 2½ cwt. of pork, beef, and most animal substances, with the addition of a comparatively small portion of salt, not only affording a considerable saving in this article, but also materially contributing to the increase of flavour and nutritive quality. Hams or beef cured this way require no previous soaking in water to being boiled, and when boiled swell in size and are extremely succulent."

"Herrings Mr. Sockett cures with very little salt. Being well dried, as early after being caught as can be effected, they are then dipped into a vat of the acid, and when dry, the same process repeated a few times, suspending them like the manufacture of candles. Mr. Sockett entertains no doubt, from the result of his experiments with herrings, that the same process would answer for other kinds of fish, as salmon, cod, &c.; and hence, when cooked, may be salted according to each individual's taste."

"I presume this acid would be found very useful on board any vessel fitted out for long voyages; it appears from calculations on a small scale, that one hogshead of this acid would suffice to cure six tons of fish, in such a manner as to retain their nutritious quality; and they could be cured on board when opportunities occurred of procuring them, independent of its being an excellent substitute for common vinegar in many culinary purposes on board."

"Mr. Sockett recommends that fish, as soon as practicable after taken, should be a little rubbed with salt, and laid upon a sloping board to drain, and when dry, to be dipped in the acid as before stated."

"One great advantage attending this mode of curing hams or beef is, that when hung up they are never attacked by the flies."

PICKLING OF FISH.

Fish may be preserved either by dry salting or in a liquid pickle. The former method is employed to a great extent on the banks of Newfoundland, and in Shetland. When a liquid pickle is used, the fish, as fresh as possible, are to be gutted, or not, and without delay plunged into the brine in quantity so as nearly to fill the reservoir, and after remaining *covered* with the pickle five or six days, they will be so completely impregnated with salt as to be perfectly fit to be re-packed in barrels, with large-grained solid salt, for the hottest climates and longest voyages.

The brine becomes frequently somewhat weaker at the top; to remedy this, some of the salt may be suspended in bags or otherwise, just under the surface, which will saturate whatever moisture may exude from the fish, and thus the whole of the brine will continue fully saturated and of the most strength.

Such brine, although repeatedly used, will not putrify, nor the fish, if kept under the surface, become rancid.

By this process great quantities of herrings may be salted when salt or casks are not on the spot, and the fish may remain for a great length of time immersed in this brine without the least injury.

From Mr. London's statement, it appears that the brine ought always to contain a redundancy of salt; and in such case there is not the least danger of the fish putrifying or growing rancid, as the extra lumps of solid salt in the brine immediately act upon any watery or other liquors which proceed from the fish when inclosed in the cask.

For judging of the relative strength of different solutions of common salt, Mr. London recommends a glass bottle, with a ground-glass stopper, to be filled with brine made from a solution of solid salt in water; within this bottle are three glass bubbles, of different specific gravities, so graduated, that supposing the temperature of the air to be at sixty degrees of Fahrenheit's thermometer, and only one bubble floats on the surface, and that it indicates the specific gravity of the brine to be 1.155, containing about 20 parts salt, and 80 of water, which is insufficient to cure animal matters with certainty by immersion in it.

When the second bubble floats, it indicates the specific gravity of the brine to be 1.180, or about 24 parts salt, and 76 parts water, which may be used for the purpose of immersion.

This brine will fully answer the purpose in the hottest weather in most climates, provided the meat or fish is always completely covered with the brine.

PICKLED MACKEREL.

After splitting the fish, and having taken off their heads and part of the skin of the belly, let them be laid in brine about three or four hours; then put them in jars with the following pickle:—two pounds common salt, two ounces saltpetre, one ounce of sugar, half ounce white pepper, one drachm corriander seed, pounded all well together; sprinkle with this mixture the bottom of the jar; then put on a layer of mackerel, with the back downwards; then a layer of the spices, and then another of mackerel, alternately, till the jar is full; press them down, and cover them close. In six months they will be ready for use.

PICKLED SALMON.

Split the fish down the middle, and divide each half into six pieces. Make a brine of salt sufficient in quantity to cover the fish when placed in a saucepan. Season with bruised pepper, mace, and allspice, and simmer the whole till the fish is done, taking care not to boil the fish more than is barely sufficient. Then take out the pieces to cool, and put them into a jar. Strain off the spice from the liquor in which the fish was boiled, and add to it a like quantity, by measure, of vinegar, and pour it over the fish. When cold, tie it over with paper, and keep the fish submersed under the liquor, by placing a weight on it.

COLLARED EELS.

Skin and bone the eels; season them with mace, chopped eschalots, pepper, salt and pimento. Roll up the whole, and tie it firmly with tape; put it in a stew-pan with a pint of veal *stock*, half pint of white wine, and half as much vinegar; and let them simmer till done. Then put them into a dish; skim off the fat, and season with salt. Clear the liquor by simmering it a few minutes, with the white of two eggs, and pass it through a cloth: after which boil it till it becomes a thick jelly when cold. Then take the tape from the eels, and pour the liquid transparent jelly over the fish.

BEST METHOD OF PRESERVING ALL KINDS OF COOKED BUTCHER'S MEAT, FISH, OR POULTRY.

Of all the methods of preserving animal substances for domestic purposes, or sea store, the process found out by Mr. Appert, and pursued in this metropolis upon a large scale by Messrs. Donkin and Gamble, is unquestionably the best. It is as follows:

Let the substance to be preserved be first par-boiled, or rather somewhat more, the bones of the meat being previously removed. Put the meat into a tin cylinder, fill up the vessel with the broth, and then solder on the lid, furnished with a small hole. When this has been done, let the tin vessel, thus prepared, be placed in water and heated to the boiling point to complete the remainder of the cooking of the meat. The hole in the lid is now closed perfectly, by soldering, whilst the air is rushing out.

The vessel is then allowed to cool, and from the diminution of volume in the contents, in consequence of the reduction of temperature, both ends of the cylinder are pressed inwards and become concave. The tin cases, thus hermetically sealed, are exposed in a *test-chamber* for at least a month, to a temperature above what they are ever likely to encounter; from 90° to 110° Fahrenheit. If the process has failed, putrefaction takes place, and gas is evolved, which in process of time will bulge out both ends of the case, so as to render them convex instead of concave. But the contents of whatever cases stand this test, will infallibly keep perfectly sweet and good in any climate, and for any length of time. If there was any taint about the meat when put up, it inevitably ferments, and is detected in the *proving* process.

All kinds of animal food may be preserved in this way—beef, mutton, veal, and poultry, either boiled or roasted. The testimonies in favour of the success of the process are of the most unexceptionable kind. At Messrs. Donkin and Gamble's establishment the meat is put up in canisters of from 4 lbs. to 20 lbs. weight each. It is charged from 1s. 8d. to 3s. a pound; roast higher than boiled, and veal dearer than mutton or beef. The weight of the canister is deducted, and nothing is charged for the canisters; and it should be observed, that these provisions being cooked, and without bone, render them equivalent to double the weight of meat in the raw state; for it is certain, that the waste in cooking, together with the weight of bone, are about one half.

Captain Neish took a quantity of provision, thus prepared, to India, not one canister spoiled; and one which he brought home contained beef in the highest state of preservation after two years, and having been carried upwards of 35,000 miles in the warmest climates.

The commissioners for victualling the navy also examined some, nearly four years old, which had been in the Mediterranean and Quebec, and found it as sound, sweet, and fresh, as if it had been only yesterday boiled. We are enabled to add the testimony of that distinguished navigator, captain Basil Hall, who has liberally communicated to us the result of his personal experience and observation, which is as follows:—"I can answer for the perfect preservation of a great number of cases which were in my possession during the voyage to China. I had 88*l.* worth, and not one failure. At that time milk was preserved in bottles corked; but tin cases have been substituted with very great effect, as I have myself tried. It is really astonishing how excellent the milk is; and, indeed, every thing preserved in this way is good."

"You must, on examining the list of prices, bear in mind, that meat thus preserved *eats* nothing, nor *drinks*—is not apt to get the rot, or to die—does not *tumble* over-board, nor get its legs broken, or its flesh wore off its bones, by knocking about the decks of a ship in bad weather—it takes no care in the keeping—it is always ready—may be eat cold or hot—and thus enables you to toss into a boat in a minute, as many days' *cooked* provisions as you choose—it is not exposed to the vicissitudes of markets, nor is it scourged up to a monstrous price (as at St. Helena), because there is no alternative. Besides these advantages, it enables one to indulge in a number of luxuries, which no care or expence *could* procure."

In this preservative process is displayed a singular and important fact with regard to the agency of oxygen in putrefaction. The tin canisters being closed during the exposure to heat, must necessarily contain with the included matter some portion of air; and if heat were not applied, or even if applied imperfectly, putrefaction would take place. This proves that the effect of the high temperature is to produce some kind of combination of the oxygen of the air with the animal or included matter, not leading to putrefaction, or even counter-acting it, while by this combination it is effectually removed. The air accordingly, where the process is successful, is deprived of oxygen; but if the heat were not sufficiently prolonged, and by far the greatest part of the air in the vessel not exhausted, putrefaction soon comes on. From experiments that have been made on this mode of preserving alimentary substances, it has been proved, that if the vessels were opened only for a short time and again closed, without heat being applied, the inclosed substances soon putrefied: as they did also from mere exposure to the air. But if, after having been exposed even for an hour or two, they were re-placed, the vessels again treated as before, and then the due degree of heat applied, they could be preserved as at first. And this repeated exposure to the air, and removal of its operation by heating, it appears from Gay Lussac's experiments, can be renewed a number of times. Nay, by occasional exposure to the heat of boiling water, without the exclusion of the air, he found the exemption from putrefaction to be attained.

The theory of these effects is not very apparent. Gay Lussac supposes, that the oxygen may combine with that principle analogous to gluten, which excites fermentation, and which may equally excite putrefaction; that this by a kind of coagulation is separated by heat, and thus rendered inert; and that it is only that part of it which has suffered oxygenation which is capable of this coagulation; it is thus removed, while the exclusion of oxygen prevents the putrefaction from taking place, which would otherwise be excited by the remainder. But this is rather hypothetical and unsatisfactory.

PRESERVATION OF MEAT BY POTTING.

The process of potting consists in reducing cooked animal substances to a pulp, by beating the meat in a mortar, and incorporating the mass with a portion of salt and spices. The pulp is then put into a jar, and covered with a thick coat of melted butter or lard, to prevent the contact of air; and the surface is further protected with a bladder-skin tied over the mouth of the jar. The muscular part of meat is best suited for potting, and the quantity of salt and spices ought to be rather liberal.

POTTED BEEF, GAME, OR POULTRY.

Take three pounds of lean beef, salt it twelve hours with half a pound of common salt, and half an ounce of saltpetre; divide it into pound pieces, and put it into an earthen pan, that will just hold it; pour in half a pint of water; cover it close with paste, and set it in a very slow oven for four hours; when it comes from the oven, pour the gravy from it into a basin, shred the meat fine, moisten it with the gravy poured from the meat, and pound it thoroughly in a marble mortar with fresh butter, till it is as fine a paste as possible, season it with black pepper and allspice, or cloves pounded, or grated nutmeg; put it in pots, press it down as close as possible; put a weight on it, and let it stand all night; next day, when it is quite cold, cover it a quarter of an inch thick with clarified butter, and tie it over with paper.

POTTED HAM.

Cut a pound of the lean of boiled ham into pieces, pound it in a mortar with fresh butter, in the proportion of about two ounces to a pound of the ham, till it is a fine paste, season it by degrees with pounded mace, pepper, and allspice; put it close down in pots, and cover it with clarified butter a quarter of an inch thick; let it stand one night in a cool place, and tie it over with paper.

Veal may be potted in a similar manner.

POTTED LOBSTER.

Take the meat and eggs from the shell; season it with powdered mace, cloves, nutmeg, pepper, salt, and anchovy liquor. Pound the meat in a marble mortar, and reduce the liquor, by evaporation, to a thick jelly; then put it and the meat together, with about one quarter of its weight of butter. Mix all together, and press it into a small pot; cover it with melted butter. When it is cold, put paper over the pots, and set them in a dry place.

Craw fish, crabs, shrimps, and prawns, may be potted in the same way.

PRESERVATION OF EGGS.

Eggs may be kept for three or four months, or more, if the pores of the shell be closed, and rendered impervious to air by some unctuous application. We generally anoint them with mutton-suet, melted, and set them on end, wedged close together, in bran, *stratum super stratum*, the containing box being closely covered.

Another method of preserving eggs is, to place them into a vessel containing lime water, or more properly slacked quicklime diluted with water, to the consistence of a thin cream, taking care that the eggs are completely covered with this liquid. The first mentioned process is, however, preferable, and answers exceedingly well.

PRESERVATIVE EFFECT OF FROST, ON BUTCHER'S MEAT, FISH, AND FOWL.

The preservative effect of frost on dead animal matter are of the utmost importance to the northern nations, by enabling them to store up a sufficient stock of all manner of animal provisions for their winter supply, and to receive stores from a great distance.

There is annually held at St. Petersburg and Moscow what is called the frozen, or winter market, for the sale of provisions solidified by frost. In a vast open square, the bodies of many thousand animals are seen on all sides, piled in pyramidal and quadrangular masses: fish, fowl, butter, eggs, hogs, sheep, deer, oxen, all rendered solid by frost. The different species of fish are strikingly beautiful; they possess the lustre and brilliancy of colour which characterises the different species in a living state.

Most of the larger kinds of quadrupeds are skinned, and classed according to their species; groups of many hundreds are piled upon their hind-legs, one against another, as if each were making an effort to climb over the back of his neighbour. The motionless, yet apparent animation of their seemingly struggling attitudes (as if they had died a sudden death), gives a horrid life to this singular scene of death. The solidity of the frozen creatures, is such, that the natives chop and saw them up, for the accommodation of the purchasers, like wood. These frozen provisions are the produce of countries very remote from each other. Siberia, Archangel, and still more distant provinces, furnish the merchandize which, during the severity of the frost, is conveyed hither on sledges.

In consequence of the multitude of these commodities, and the short period allowed to the existence of the market, they are cheaper than at any other time of the year, and are, therefore, purchased in larger quantities, to be stored, as a winter stock.

When disposed in cellars, they will keep, with care, for a considerable time during the cold season. All the provisions which remain, and are exposed to the temperate atmosphere, speedily putrify; but as the desertion of the frost is generally pretty well calculated, almost to a day, but little loss is suffered in this respect. The same advantage is taken of the cold in Canada, and all other countries, when the frost is sufficiently steady.

Substances, so long as they are hard frozen, probably undergo no chemical change, of which the most striking proof was afforded by the body of an animal, probably antediluvian, being found imbedded in a mass of ice at the mouth of the Lena; but in the act of freezing, or of the subsequent thawing, some alteration is produced, which affects the nature of the substance. This may be either merely mechanical, from the particles of ice during their formation, tearing asunder and separating the fibres, or chemical, by destroying the intimate union of the constituents of the fluids, as in wine injured by having been frozen; or by causing new combinations, of which we have an example in the sweetness acquired by the potatoe.

Captain Scoresby, contrary to popular belief, states, that "the most surprising action of the frost, on fresh provision, is in preserving it a long time from putrefaction, even after it is thawed and returns into a warm climate.[34] I have," says he, "eaten unsalted mutton and beef nearly five months old, which has been constantly exposed to a temperature above the freezing point for four or five weeks in the outset, and occasionally assailed by the septical influences of rain, fog, heat, and electricity, and yet it has proved perfectly sweet. It may be remarked, that unsalted meat that has been preserved four or five months in a cold climate, and then brought back to the British coasts during the warmth of summer, must be consumed very speedily after it is cut into, or it will fail in a day or two. It will seldom, indeed, keep sweet after being cooked above twenty or thirty hours."

> [34] Account of the Arctic Regions, with a History and Description of the Northern Whale Fishery.

In freezing animal substances, for the purpose of preserving them, no other precaution is necessary than exposing them to a sufficient degree of cold. "Animal substances," says Captain Scoresby, "requisite as food, of all descriptions (fish excepted), may be taken to Greenland and there preserved any length of time, without being smoked, dried, or salted. No preparation of any kind is necessary for their preservation; nor is any other precaution requisite, excepting suspending them in the air when taken on shipboard, shielding them a little from the sun and wet, and immersing them occasionally in sea-water, or throwing sea-water over them after heavy rains, which will effectually prevent putrescency on the outward passage; and, in Greenland, the cold becomes a sufficient preservation, by freezing them as hard as blocks of wood. The moisture is well preserved by freezing, a little from the surface only evaporating; so that if cooked when three, four, or five months old, meat will frequently appear as profuse of gravy, as if it had been but recently killed." Captain Scoresby has not informed us why fish cannot be taken to Greenland in a frozen state, though this is a mode of preservation much used in Russia and Germany, and even in this country.

Some attention is necessary for thawing provisions which have been frozen. "When used, the beef cannot be divided but by an axe or saw; the latter instrument is preferred. It is then put into cold water, from which it derives heat by the formation of ice around it, and soon thaws; but if put into hot water, much of the gravy is extracted, and the meat is injured without being thawed more readily. If an attempt be made to cook it before it is thawed, it may be burnt on the outside, while the centre remains raw, or actually in a frozen state." These observations, which we have transcribed from Captain Scoresby, an excellent observer, agree with the directions of earlier writers. Thus Krünitz says,[35] "when fish taken under the ice are frozen, lay them in cold water, which thus draws the ice out of the fish, so that it can be scraped off their scales. They taste much better afterwards than when they are allowed to thaw in a warm room."

[35] Encyclop. Vol. X. p. 586.

Pickles.

The antiseptic power of vinegar is employed with advantage in domestic economy for preserving from decay a variety of fruits, roots, leaves, and other parts of vegetables, which by a species of refinement and luxury, are often considered as condiments to improve the relish of several kinds of food. Their qualities, no doubt, depends almost entirely on the vinegar, spice, or salt imbibed by them.

The art of preparing vinegar pickles consists in impregnating the vegetable substances with the strongest vinegar, to which are usually added a portion of common salt, and the most heating spices. To effect this object, the substance to be pickled is usually suffered to macerate, or slightly boiled with the acid, and afterwards kept infused in it, together with spices and salt.

It is customary to impregnate the article to be pickled first in a strong brine of common salt; but this is not absolutely necessary for the preservation of the pickled substance. To facilitate the action of the vinegar or salt, the articles to be pickled, especially such as walnuts, cucumbers, &c. should be punctured with a large needle or fork. To assist their preservation, and to improve their flavour, a variety of pungent and aromatic spices are added, which vary according to the fancy of the cook; pepper, pimento, cloves, mace, ginger, capsicum, and mustard, are the spices usually employed.

For the preparation of acid pickles, the vinegar prepared from wood, as in itself containing no substance liable to a spontaneous decay, is preferable to common malt vinegar, although the contrary has been asserted, because it is free from mucilage, which promotes the spoiling of common vinegar, and therefore the former is a better antiseptic than vinegar abounding in mucilage. We prepare our home-made pickles with this acid, and we are authorised to state that, although kept for years, they are inferior to none met with in commerce.

All pickles should be preserved in unglazed earthenware jars, carefully corked, and tied over with a bladder to exclude air. The vinegar used for preparing them should always be heated in an unglazed earthenware pan, it should never be suffered to boil, but poured over the substance to be pickled, just when it begins to simmer. The spices may be simmered with the vinegar.

PICKLED RED CABBAGE.

Put sliced red cabbage into a stone jar, and strew amongst it common salt; then heat vinegar nearly to a boiling point, and pour it over the cabbage, in a sufficient quantity to cover the sliced leaves. It is customary to add long pepper, allspice, and ginger, to the vinegar, which impart to the pickle a pungent taste. A small quantity of powdered cochineal is also frequently added, with an intent to give to the cabbage a beautiful red colour; the cochineal should be strewed amongst the sliced leaves previous to the infusion of the vinegar; two drachms are sufficient to one pound of cabbage. Red beet root is employed for a similar purpose, but the former pigment, which is perfectly harmless, is preferable. When the pickle is cold, it should be tied over with a bladder skin to exclude the air.

PICKLED ONIONS.

For this pickle the small white round onions, of the size of a child's playing marble, are usually chosen. Having peeled off the exterior brown coat of the onions, simmer them in water, till their outer layers have acquired a semi-transparency, (not longer), then strain off the water, and suffer the onions to dry; put them into an unglazed earthen jar and pour over them so much colourless vinegar, previously heated nearly to the boiling point, as will cover them. The seasoning spices usually added are white pepper, ginger root, white mustard seed, mace, and salt.

PICKLED WALNUTS.

Take unripe walnuts; run a large needle through each in several places; suffer them to macerate for ten or twelve days, in a strong brine of common salt. When this has been done, decant the brine, transfer the walnuts into a stone jar, and pour vinegar, previously heated nearly to the boiling point, over them, in a sufficient quantity to cover them.

They may be seasoned with long pepper, capsicum, ginger, mustard seed, mace, and pimento. These substances should be simmered with the vinegar for a few minutes.

The walnuts will not be fit for use till when about six months old.

PICKLED CUCUMBERS.

Perforate fresh gathered cucumbers, with a needle, or fork, put them into a stone jar, and pour over them boiling hot vinegar. Season with salt, pimento, long pepper, and ginger. These substances should be simmered with the vinegar for a few minutes.

To this pickle is sometimes intentionally given a lively green colour, by copper, and numerous fatal consequences are known to have ensued from the use of such a practice.[36]

> [36] Treatise on the Adulteration of Food and Culinary Poisons, 1821.—"Poisonous Pickles."

If pickled cucumber, or any other kind of vegetable pickle, be wanted of a lively green colour, it may readily be effected by soaking them when ready prepared, for a few minutes, first in tincture of turmeric, and then in a diluted solution of the colouring matter of indigo, dissolved in water.[37] This method of straining the pickle is perfectly harmless.

> [37] This substance is called, at the colour-shops, intense (not liquid blue, which is quite a different preparation of Indigo,) blue.

Samphire, French beans, tomatoes, capsicum pods, nasturtium and raddish pods, may be pickled in the same manner.

PICKLED RED BEET-ROOT.

Boil the root till sufficiently done; peel it and cut it into thin slices. Put it into a stone jar, and pour over it white vinegar, seasoned with long pepper, horse-raddish, cut into small slices, allspice, cloves, and salt.

PICKLED MUSHROOMS.

Having peeled small button mushrooms, put them in a strong brine of salt for three or four days; strain off the brine, and pour over them boiling hot vinegar: season with long pepper, ginger, and mace.

PICKLED ARTICHOKE.

Take large fresh gathered artichokes, boil and simmer them till they are nearly tender, remove the leaves and choke, and put the bottom part of the artichoke in a salt brine for about forty-eight hours; then strain off the brine, put the artichoke into a jar, and cover it with vinegar, previously heated to the boiling point, and seasoned with pepper, salt, eschalots, and mace.

SOUR KRAUT.

M. Parmentier has given a minute description of a process of making sour kraut on the large scale. The heads of white winter cabbages, after removing the outer leaves, are to be cut into fine shreds, by means of a knife, or with a plane, and spread out to dry upon a cloth in the shade. A cask is to be set on end, with the head taken out. If it formerly contained vinegar or wine, so much the better, as it will promote the fermentation, and give the cabbage a more vinous taste; if not, the inside may be rubbed over with sour kraut liquor. Caraway seeds are to be mixed with the shreds of cabbage, a good layer of salt is placed at the bottom of the cask, and then cabbage shreds evenly packed, to the depth of four or six inches. The layers are regularly stamped down with a wooden stamper, to half their original bulk. The same process is to be repeated, with additional layers of salt, and shreds, till the whole be packed. They are then to be covered with a layer of salt, or till the barrel be filled within two inches of the top, over which the outside leaves of the cabbages are to be spread. About two pounds of salt are required for twenty middling sized cabbages.

The head of the barrel, which should have been previously well fastened together, is lastly to be put within the barrel above the leaves, and loaded with stones, to prevent the mixture from rising during the fermentation. The mass thus compressed subsides, and the cabbage gives out its juice, which rises to the surface, it is green, muddy, and fætid. It is to be drawn off by a spigot placed two or three inches from the bottom, and re-placed by fresh brine.

The following notice may serve to remind the reader of the time when the various articles for preparing pickles are in season.

Nasturtium pods fit for pickling, are in season in the middle of July.
Onions, by the middle and end of July.
Cucumbers, the latter part of July and August.
Capsicum pods, the end of July and beginning of August.
Tomatas, or Love Apples, the end of July and August.
Cauliflower, in July and August.
Artichokes, in July and August.
Radish pods, in July.
French Beans, in July.
Mushrooms, in September.
Red Cabbage, in August.
Samphire, in August.

MUSHROOM CATSUP.

The name of catsup is given to several kinds of liquid pickles, made of savoury vegetable substances, such as mushrooms, walnuts, &c. The following method of preparing mushroom catsup is copied from the Cook's Oracle:—

Take full grown mushrooms; put a layer of them at the bottom of a deep earthen pan, and sprinkle them with salt, then another layer of mushrooms, put some more salt on them, and so on, alternately, salt and mushrooms; let them remain two or three hours, by which time the salt will have penetrated the mushrooms, and rendered them easy to break; mash them well and let them remain for a couple of days, stirring them up, and mashing them well each day; then pour them into a stone jar, and to each quart add half an ounce of whole black pepper; stop the jar very close, set it in a stew-pan of boiling water, and keep it simmering for two hours at least. Take out the jar, and pour off the juice clear from the sediment through a hair sieve into a stewpan (without squeezing the mushrooms); let it boil up, skim it, and pour it into a dry jar; let it stand till next day, then pour it off as gently as possible, through a tammis, or flannel bag, (so as not to disturb the sediment at the bottom of the jar.) Bottle it in pints or half pints; for it is best to keep it in such quantities as are soon used: in each pint, put a dozen berries of black pepper, the same of allspice, and a table-spoonful of brandy.

TOMATA CATSUP.

Mash a gallon of ripe tomatas; add to it one pound of salt, press out the juice, and to each quart add a quarter of a pound of anchovies, two ounces of eshallots, and an ounce of ground black pepper; simmer the mixture for a quarter of an hour; then strain it through a sieve, and put to it a quarter of an ounce of pounded mace, the same quantity of allspice, ginger, and nutmeg, and half a drachm of cochineal; let the whole simmer for twenty minutes, and strain it through a bag: when cold, bottle it:

Or, put tomatas into an earthen pan, and bake them very slowly in an oven. Rub the pulp through a hair sieve, to separate the seeds and skins. To every pound, by weight, of the pulp, add a pint and a quarter of vinegar, with a drachm of mace, ginger, cloves, allspice, and one ounce each of white pepper, and minced eshallot. Simmer them for half an hour, and strain off the liquid.

WALNUT CATSUP.

Take 28 lbs. of unripe walnuts when quite tender, reduce them to a pulp in a marble mortar; add to the mass two gallons of vinegar; let it stand three or four days; to each gallon of liquor, put a quarter of a pound of minced eshallots, half an ounce of bruised cloves, the same of mace and black pepper, one tea-spoonful of Cayenne pepper, and a quarter of a pound of salt: give it a boil up, and strain it through a flannel.

Conserved Fruits.

The preserving of the pulpy fruits employed in housekeeping for making fruit pies, tarts and puddings, so as to render them fit for that purpose, when they cannot be procured in their recent state, is an object of considerable importance in every well regulated family.

The expence of sugar is frequently urged as a reason for not conserving fruits in housekeeping, and to this may be added the uncertainty of success from the strong fermentable quality of many fruits, if the sugar has not been very liberally added. They may indeed be conserved for a length of time without sugar, by baking them in an oven, and then closely stopping them up; but if the cork becomes dry, the atmospheric air exchanges place with what is impregnated by the fruit, which then soon becomes mouldy; some pulpy fruits may be conserved in good condition by the following method, for years, or even it is probable for a longer period, in hot climates.

CONSERVATION OF RECENT FRUITS WITHOUT SUGAR.

The following fruits may be conserved without sugar. The more juicy fruits of the berry kind, such as currants, mulberries, strawberries, raspberries, are not well calculated for this process.

METHOD OF CONSERVING GOOSEBERRIES,

Orlean Plums	Peaches
Green Gages	Nectarines
Damsons	Bullaces.

Let the fruit be clean picked, and not too ripe, put it into wide-mouthed, or what are called gooseberry bottles, let the bottles be filled as full as they can be packed, and stick the corks lightly into them; then place them upright in a saucepan of water, heated gradually to about 100 or 170° F. that is, until the water feels very hot to the finger, but does not scald. Let this degree of heat be kept up for half an hour, then remove the bottles one by one, and fill them up to within half an inch of the cork with boiling water; when cold let the cork be fitted very close, and lay the bottles on their sides, that the cork may be kept moist by the water. To prevent fermentation and mould, the bottles must be turned once or twice a week for the first month or two, and once or twice a month afterwards. When applied to use, some of the liquor first poured off may serve to be put into the pie, or pudding, instead of water, and the remainder being boiled up with a little sugar, makes a rich and agreeable syrup.

The fruit ought not be cracked by the heat; some trials were made by keeping the bottles in a heat of 190° for three quarters of an hour, but the fruit was reduced nearly to a pulp. It is also advisable that the fruit be not quite ripe, nor should it be bruised.

Some fruits may be preserved in a succulent state by being kept in water, without boiling. This is practised in regard to the cranberry: it also succeeds with the smaller kinds of apples. All pulpy fruits, such as damsons, plums, &c., if gathered when not quite ripe, and not wounded, may likewise be preserved, by putting them into dry bottles, so as to exclude the air, by sealing over the cork, and then burying them in a trench, with the cork downwards.

CONSERVATION OF RECENT FRUITS, BY MEANS OF SUGAR, IN A LIQUID STATE.

A great number of fruits in their natural state may be conserved in a fluid, transparent syrup, of such a consistence as will prevent them from spoiling. This method of conserving fruits requires some care; for if they are too little impregnated with sugar, they do not keep, and if the syrup is too concentrated, the sugar crystallizes, and thus spoils the conserved fruit.

METHOD OF CONSERVING APRICOTS BY MEANS OF SUGAR.

Plums
Damsons
Green Gages

Peaches
Nectarines.

Take apricots, not too ripe, cut a small slit near the stem end of the fruit, and push out the stone; simmer them in water till nearly half done, then peel them, and simmer them again for about twenty minutes in a syrup, made of two parts by measure of water, and one part by weight of loaf sugar. When this has been done, put them aside for about twelve hours; strain off the syrup, and to one pint of it add four ounces of lump sugar, simmer the fruit again for about ten minutes in this concentrated syrup; skim off the impurities that rise to the surface, and repeat the simmering of the fruit in the syrup three or four times; and, lastly, put the apricots into pots, and cover them with a syrup made of seven ounces, by measure, of water, and one pound of loaf sugar. Tie over or cork the jar to exclude the air.

CONSERVED PINE APPLES.

Break off the top and stalk of the pine apple, cut the fruit into slices, about one-fifth of an inch in thickness; put the slices into an earthenware jar, at the bottom of which has been previously put a layer of powdered lump sugar, about one-eighth of an inch in thickness. Place on this stratum of sugar, a layer of the slices of the fruit, then put another layer of sugar, and so on; lastly, put the jar up to the neck into a saucepan of boiling water, and keep the water boiling for about half an hour, or till the sugar is completely dissolved, taking care to remove the scum that rises on the surface. Tie over the mouth of the jar with a wet bladder, or keep it well corked.

CONSERVED PEARS.

Put peeled pears in a stone pan with water, let them simmer till they are soft, skim them, and when cold simmer them for about ten minutes in a syrup made of three parts by measure, of water, and one by weight of loaf sugar, let them remain in the syrup till the next day; then pour off the syrup from the pears, simmer them again for about ten minutes, and repeat the simmering in the syrup three or four times successively. They are usually coloured red by powdered cochineal, a small portion of which is added during the boiling process. Some persons add cinnamon, and other spices, and a portion of port wine. If the pears be not intended to keep, they may be simmered till done in a syrup, composed of one pound of sugar and three pints and a half of water.

CONSERVATION OF RECENT FRUITS, BY MEANS OF SUGAR, IN A SOLID FORM.

The name of *candied fruits*, or *comfits*, is given to such substances as are preserved by means of sugar in a solid state, so that the whole substance is impregnated and covered with sugar, in a crystalline, or solid state.

CANDIED ORANGE, OR LEMON PEEL.

Soak Seville orange peel, well cleaned from the pulp in several waters, till it loses its bitterness; cut it into thin slips, simmer them in a syrup composed of two parts, by weight, of lump sugar, and one of water, and continue the simmering till they are become tender, and nearly transparent. Then take them out, put them aside for about twenty-four hours; and simmer them again in a sufficient quantity of a syrup composed of six ounces, by measure, of water, and one pound of loaf sugar, and continue the simmering till the sugar candies about the pan and peel. Now lay them separately on a wire sieve to drain; sift finely powdered sugar over them, whilst still hot, and put them to dry in a warm stove.

Candied lemon peel may be prepared in the same manner.

Marmalades, Jams,
AND
Fruit Pastes.

Marmalades, Fruit Jams, and Pastes, are compositions of the pulpy matter of recent Fruits, or other vegetable substances, so combined into a mass with sugar, as will cause them to suffer as little alteration as possible in their native qualities. These comfitures are therefore in reality solid extracts of the pulpy matter of fruit conserved by means of sugar.

The evaporation of the mass is most conveniently performed in broad hollow vessels; the larger the surface of the vessel, the sooner will the aqueous parts exhale. When the pulpy matter begins to grow thick, great care is necessary to prevent its burning. This accident is almost unavoidable if the quantity be large, and the fire applied, as usual, under the pan; it may be effectually prevented, by pouring the mass, when it has acquired the consistence of syrup, into shallow earthen pans, and placing those in an oven with its door open, moderately heated; which, acting uniformly on every part of the liquid, will soon reduce it to any degree of consistence required. This may likewise be done, and more securely, by setting the evaporating vessels in boiling water; but the evaporation is in this way very tedious. The application of steam by means of what is called a *preserving pan*, is the best contrivance for preparing jams, fruit pastes, and all other culinary preparations, which are liable to become injured by a degree of heat exceeding that of boiling water.

BLACK CURRANT PASTE.

Mash the currants in a bowl or marble mortar, so as to break all the berries without materially bruising the seeds; put the mass into a saucepan, and heat it nearly to the boiling point; then rub it through a sieve to separate the seeds. To one pint measure of the pulpy juice, add one pound and a half of loaf sugar, let the mixture simmer gently over the fire, and keep stirring it to prevent it burning at the bottom of the pan. Continue the simmering till the mass, when cold, assumes the consistence of a stiff, or almost solid paste, which may be readily known by placing from time to time a tea spoonful of it on a cold plate. When the mass has acquired the proper consistence, pour it out on a marble slab, or earthenware plate, and continue the further exsiccation by putting it in a stove, or on a hot hearth.

APRICOT PASTE,

Peach Paste   Cherry Paste
Plum Paste   Quince Paste.

Take ripe apricots, boil them till quite soft, mash them, and rub the mass through a splinter sieve, put the pulp into a pan, and to every pound put half a pound of powdered loaf sugar; put it again on the fire to simmer till the paste drops off easily from the spoon, then take it from the fire and pour it on a slab.

Peach, quince, plum, and cherry paste, may be prepared in the same manner.

RASPBERRY PASTE.

Mash the raspberries, and having heated the mass in a saucepan, pass it through a splinter sieve; simmer the mass gently to the consistence of a paste, and to every pound and a quarter of the pulp, add one pound and a half of powdered loaf sugar, and proceed as before directed.—*See black currant paste.*

ORANGE AND LEMON PASTE.

Squeeze out the juice of Seville oranges, and boil the rinds in water till they are tender enough to be crushed between the finger; scoop out the pulp of the fruit, and put it aside; pound the rind, in a mortar, to form a smooth mass, pass it through a splinter sieve; add to it the juice, and keep it on the fire till the mass acquires the consistence of a paste; then take it off, weigh it, and to every pound and a quarter add two pounds of powdered loaf sugar; mix and finish it like black currant paste. *See page 260*.

Lemon paste is made in a like manner.

RASPBERRY JAM.

Strawberry Jam Gooseberry Jam
　Currant Jam Mulberry Jam.

Having mashed the raspberries, put them into a saucepan, and make them boiling hot; rub the pulp through a coarse splinter sieve, and to a pint, by measure, add one pound of powdered loaf sugar; simmer the mixture with a gentle heat till the mass has acquired the consistence of a stiff paste, and comes off from the bottom of the pan, taking care to stir the mixture continually with a wooden spatula when it begins to thicken. Put the jam into pots, which should be perfectly dry, for the least damp spoils it. When quite cold, tie it over.

Strawberry, currant, gooseberry, and mulberry jam, may be prepared in a like manner.

APRICOT JAM.

Take ripe apricots, cut them into pieces, and remove the stones; mash the fruit in a marble mortar, to form it into a smooth pulp; heat it over the fire, and when nearly boiling hot, rub it through a splinter sieve; add to one pint, by measure, of the pulp, one pound of powdered sugar; stir the mixture together, and suffer it to simmer over the fire till it comes clear from the bottom of the pan, taking care to stir the mixture all the time.

ORANGE MARMALADE.

Marmalades scarcely differ from jams. This name is applied to those comfitures which are composed of the firmer fruits, such as quinces, pine-apples, &c.; whereas jams are made of the more juicy, esculent berries, such as strawberries, currants, mulberries, &c.

Cut the oranges into pieces, remove the pulp, squeeze it through a sieve, and measure it. Boil the rind in water till it is quite soft, then clear it from the interior side of the white pulpy mass, so that nothing but the thin outer yellow rind is left. To every pint of the pulpy juice add three-quarters of a pound of coarsely powdered loaf sugar, and add also the rind of the yellow orange, cut into thin slips. Let the whole simmer, till a sample, when taken out of the saucepan, and suffered to cool on a plate, exhibits the consistence of a semi-fluid mass.

PEACH MARMALADE.

Peel the peaches and take out the stones, simmer them till half done, then drain them, reduce them to a pulp, and squeeze the mass through a coarse splinter sieve. Weigh the pulp, and to every pound add twelve ounces of powdered loaf sugar; simmer the mass till it has acquired a stiff pasty consistence.

PINE APPLE MARMALADE.

Cut the fruit into small pieces, pound it in a mortar, and pass the mass through a coarse splinter sieve; weigh the pulp, and add to every pound three-quarters of a pound of powdered loaf sugar, and six ounces of water, and simmer it as before described.

APRICOT MARMALADE.

Boil ripe apricots in water till they can be crushed between the fingers, then take them out, extract the stones, reduce the fruit to a pulp, and pass the mass through a sieve; weigh the pulp, and to every pound take three-quarters of a pound of loaf sugar; simmer it till it hangs on the spoon, like a stiff jelly. Quince marmalade may be prepared in a like manner.

FRUIT JELLIES

Are compounds of the juices of fruits combined with sugar, concentrated by boiling to such a consistence, that the liquid, upon cooling, assumes the form of a tremulous glue.

In the preparation of jellies, care must be taken not to boil it too long, as it looses by this means the property of gelatinising, and assumes the form of mucilage, the danger of this is greatest when the quantity of sugar is too small to absorb the water of the juice.

Fruit jellies should not be kept in glazed earthenware pots, because they act, or dissolve a portion of the glaze. They should (and all other comfitures) be covered with paper dipped in brandy, and the pots should be tied over with paper.

CURRANT JELLY.

Mash the currants, and pass them through a splinter sieve, put the pulp on the fire, stir it with a spoon till it begins to boil, then strain the mass through a flannel bag to render the juice clear; measure it, and to a pint put one pound and a half of loaf sugar, and let it simmer very gently, till you see, by dipping a spoon or skimmer in the jelly, and again raising it, the jelly forms a web upon it, which, if simmered enough, will remain on the skimmer. Then take it off the fire, let it stand a few minutes till the scum has collected on the surface, remove it and put the clear fluid into pots. When quite cold, cut pieces of writing paper to the size of the brim of the pots, steep the paper in brandy and place it on the jelly.

RASPBERRY JELLY.

The juice of this fruit does not gelatinize readily on account of the quantity of mucilage which it contains; hence, for preparing a jelly by means of this fruit, it is necessary to add to one part of raspberries at least two parts of red or white currant juice. The jelly may then be obtained by following the directions stated for making currant jelly.

BARBERRY JELLY.

Pick the barberries from the stalks, mash them, and having heated the mass in a saucepan throw it into a flannel bag, to strain off the juice. To one pint of the clear juice add one pound and a half of loaf sugar, simmer it with a gentle heat till it gelatinizes.

GOOSEBERRY JELLY.

Take two quarts of bruised gooseberries, simmer the mass with one pint and a half of water for about a quarter of an hour, then put it into a flannel bag to strain off the juice, and to one pint add one pound and a half of lump sugar; simmer it, as stated under the article currant jelly.

APPLE JELLY.

Pare four pounds of russettins or any other sub-acid apples, cut them into small pieces, and boil them in two quarts of water, till they become quite soft, then put them into a sieve, strain off the liquid, and run it through a flannel bag to render it clear; measure it, and to one pint of the liquid add one pound and a half of sugar, and finish the jelly as before directed. *See Currant Jelly.*

QUINCE AND APRICOT JELLY

May be prepared in a similar manner.

FRUIT SYRUPS.

A weak syrup has a tendency to ferment and quickly become sour if kept in a temperate degree of heat; it is therefore not calculated to prevent the natural fermentation of vegetable juices, which always increase its tendency to corrupt. Pharmaceutists have ascertained that a solution, prepared by dissolving two parts of double refined sugar in one of water, or any watery fluid, and boiling the solution a little, forms a syrup, which neither ferments nor crystallizes; and this proportion may be considered as the basis of all syrups, and seems to be the degree of boiling syrup called *smooth* by the confectioners.

After having squeezed the fruit for the syrup, leave the mass for several days undisturbed: a slight fermentation takes place, this will separate the mucilage and thick parenchyma which rendered the juice viscid. By degrees these matters subside, and very often the liquor appears perfectly clear. This liquor may be separated by decantation: put the remaining matter under the press, and by these means a juice not so clear as the preceding is obtained, but which easily becomes clear spontaneously, especially if put into bottles immediately on its being expressed, and suffered to ferment during some days; by this means a transparent juice of the fruit is obtained.

LEMON SYRUP.

Take a pint of fresh lemon juice, add to it two pounds of lump sugar; simmer it for a few minutes, and remove the scum till the surface is quite clean, then add an ounce of thin cut lemon-peel; let them all simmer very gently for a few minutes, and strain it through a flannel. When cool, bottle, and keep it in a cool place.

ORANGE SYRUP.

Squeeze the oranges, and strain the juice from the pulp; to a pint of the juice, add two pounds of sugar; give it a boil, skim it well, strain it through a flannel, and let it stand till cold, and then bottle it.

MULBERRY SYRUP.

Take Mulberry juice strained, rendered clear by having suffered it to ferment, as directed page 273, one pint; add to it refined sugar, two pounds; simmer the sugar in the juice, and proceed as directed.—*See Currant Syrup.*

RASPBERRY AND CURRANT SYRUP

May be prepared in a like manner.

PRESERVATION AND STORING OF FRUIT,—PRINCIPAL REQUISITES OF A GOOD FRUIT ROOM.

In storing fruits, care should be taken not to bruise them. Pears, apples, and all other summer fruit should be placed on shelves singly in a dry and well aired room, and not on moss, hay, or straw, as is often done, because they thereby contract a very disagreeable flavour. It is better to lay the fruit on a clean shelf, covered with a sheet of common writing paper; brown paper gives them a flavour of pitch.

The finer large kinds of pears should not be allowed to touch one another, but should be laid single and distinct. Apples, and all kinds of pears, should be laid thin; never tier above tier, which causes them to sweat, and undergo a kind of fermentation, which renders them mealy. A great deal of the preservation of summer fruit depends on the manner of gathering them. After having prepared the fruit-room, a fine day is to be chosen, and, if possible, after two or three preceding days of dry weather, and about two in the afternoon the fruit is to be gathered, and deposited in baskets of a moderate size, taking care that none of it receive any bruise or blemish, for the injured part soon rots and spoils the sound fruit in contact with it. As the summer fruits ripen more quickly after they are pulled, only a few days' consumption should be gathered at once. Autumn apples and pears should be gathered about eight days before they are ripe, and indeed some kinds never become fit for eating on the tree. If they have been necessarily gathered in wet weather, or early in the morning, they should be exposed a day to the sun to dry, and they should on no account be wiped, which rubs off the *bloom,* as it is called, which, when allowed to dry, on some fruits, constitutes a natural varnish, closing up the pores, and preventing the evaporation of the juices.

Fine pears may be preserved by passing a thread through the stack, and having sealed up the end of the stack with a drop of sealing wax, to hang them up separately in a cone of paper, suspended by the thread.

Grapes keep much better when hanging than when laid upon a table, and it is advisable also to seal the cut end with a drop of sealing wax; or they may be hung by the stack, or by the point of the bunch, as the grapes are thus less pressed against each other; but it is in both cases necessary to visit them from time to time, and to cut off with a pair of scissors every berry that is mouldy or spoiled.

More artificial modes of preserving grapes in a succulent state are sometimes used, and become necessary for their transportation to distant countries. They are often packed with bran and saw dust. If intended for transportation they should not be quite ripe.

The principal requisites of a good fruit room are great dryness and equality of temperature, and the power of excluding light. It should be furnished with a number of shallow trays, supported on a rack or stand one above another. It should have openings to admit fresh air during fine weather. It should be warmed during frost.

PRESERVATION OF RECENT ESCULENT ROOTS, POT-HERBS, AND OTHER CULINARY VEGETABLES.

When it is necessary to keep vegetables a few days before they are made use of, care should be taken that they receive as little injury as possible from keeping. The rules are simple and easy:—vegetables of different sorts should not be left in the same bundle, or basket; they should not be washed till they are about to be used; but if they have got flaccid, or dry-shrivelled, and wrinkly, (not otherwise,) they should be immersed in water: but to prevent them becoming so, the best method is not to expose them to the sun or air, but to keep them in a cool, dark, damp place, not scattered about, but close together, though not in great quantities, lest they heat, and a sort of fermentation begins, which destroys the quality altogether.—Strong scented vegetables should be kept apart from those that are inodorous.

Leeks or cellery will quickly spoil a whole basketful of cauliflower, sallads, or the finer vegetables.

Another general rule, as already stated, is, that they should not be kept in water when fresh, or refreshed by sprinkling them with water, (as is often practised,) till they are to be used, for the flavour is thereby greatly injured. It is only when they have become flaccid that they should be immersed in water to restore their crispness before they are cooked, otherwise they will be tough and unpalatable; this is to be done, when the size of the vegetable admits of it, as cauliflower, sallad, cellery, &c., by cutting off a piece of the stalk and setting the fresh surface, thus exposed, in water, which will be absorbed; in other cases the whole vegetable must be immersed in water.

Most vegetable substances being more or less succulent, their full proportion of fluids is necessary for their retaining that state of crispness or plumpness which they have when growing. On being cut or gathered the exhalation from their surface continues, while, from the open vessels of the cut surface, there is often great exudation or evaporation, and thus their natural moisture is diminished, and the tender leaves become flaccid, and the thicker masses or roots lose their plumpness. This is not only less pleasant to the eye, but is a real injury to the nutritious powers of the vegetable; for in this flaccid and shrivelled state its fibres are less easily divided in chewing, and the water which exists in vegetable substances, in the form of their respective natural juices, is directly nutritious. The first care in the preservation of succulent vegetables, therefore, is to prevent them from losing their natural moisture. In regard to the tender succulent vegetables this is not altogether possible; because there is a constant exhalation from their surface, while the supply of moisture is cut off. The principle of preserving them, then, is to retard and diminish the exhalation. Even growing vegetables become flaccid in a hot sun, because the exhalation is then greater than the supply; and exposure to the sun is absolutely ruinous to all the more delicate vegetables.—The operation of heat and air is slower but similar. Succulent vegetables should, therefore, be kept in a cool, shady, and damp place.

Common sense will suggest what is best, when it is known that to keep vegetables fresh for a short time, the best way is to hinder them from becoming too dry, and therefore to keep them from heat and air, and to avoid crushing or bruising them.

If they become frozen in the cold of winter, they should be immersed in cold water for an hour or two, and the water should be changed once or twice.

The earthy mould should never be washed from potatoes, or any other sort of roots, till they are to be dressed.

When potatoes, turnips, carrots, or any other roots are to be preserved for a length of time, they should be covered with earth, or straw and mats, to preserve them both from the air and the action of frost, which is peculiarly hurtful to all vegetable substances.

Sweet herbs, or savoury pot-herbs should be gathered in a dry day. Cleanse them well from dirt and dust, cut off the roots, separate the bunches into smaller ones, and hang them across a line in the kitchen, where there is a moderate heat, which will dry them in an excellent manner: when perfectly dry, put them in bags, and lay them by on a shelf in the kitchen, they will keep good for twelve months, and be ready in the moment when wanted: or rub off the stalks, put them through a coarse hair sieve, and put the powder into stopped bottles; by this means their flavour is still better preserved.—They are in the highest state of perfection just before they begin to flower; the first and last crop have neither the fine flavour nor the perfume of those which are gathered in the height of the season; that is when the greater part of the crop of each species is ripe at the same period.

Basil is in the best state for drying from the middle and end of August.
Knotted Marjoram, from the beginning of July, and during the whole month.
Winter Savory, the latter end of July, and throughout August.
Summer Savory, the latter end of July, and throughout August.
Thyme, *Lemon-Thyme*, and *Orange-Thyme*, during June and July.
Mint, the latter part of June, and during July.
Sage, in August and September.
Tarragon, in June, July, August.

Tea.

The dried leaves of the tea plant, a commodity with which we are so well acquainted, and which affords a beverage so generally used in this country, must excite curiosity to know something of its natural history, or the nature of the plant from which it is obtained.

The precise period when tea was first made known in Europe cannot be ascertained; it is said that some Dutch adventurers, seeking for such objects as might fetch a high price in China, and hearing of the general use there of a beverage from a plant of that country, made them fall upon the idea of trying whether not an European plant might be relished by the Chinese, and become an article of commerce among them, and accordingly they introduced to them the herb *Sage*, the adventurers accepting in return the Chinese tea, which they brought to Europe. The European herb did not continue long in use in China, but the consumption of tea has been amazingly increasing in Europe ever since. It is generally said, that it was first imported from Holland into England, about 1666, by lord Arlington and lord Ossory, who brought it into fashion among people of quality. But it was used in coffee-houses before this period, as it appears by an act of parliament made in 1660, in which a duty of 8*d.* was laid on every gallon of the infusion sold in these places. In 1666 it was sold in London for 60*s.* per pound, though it did not cost more than 2*s.* 6*d.* or 3*s.* 6*d.* at Batavia. It continued at this price till 1700. In 1715 green tea began to be used; and as great quantities were then imported, the price was lessened, and the practice of drinking tea descended to the lower ranks. In 1720, the French began to send tea to us by a clandestine commerce. Since that period the demand has been increasing yearly, and it has become almost a necessary of life in several parts of Europe, even among the lowest as well as the highest ranks.

NATURAL HISTORY OF THE TEA TREE.

The tea tree (Polyandria Monogynia) is a native of China, Japan, and Tonquin, it has never been found growing wild in any other country. Linnæus says, that there are two species of this plant, the Bohe´a, or black, and the Vir´idis, or green tea. The green has much longer leaves than the black, it is a more hardy plant; and, with very little protection, bears the severity of our winters. The tea is planted in China round borders of fields, without regard to the soil.

The tree attains the height of ten or twelve feet, and is an evergreen: the leaves, which are the only valuable part of it, are about an inch and a half long, and resemble those of sweet brier. The flowers are something like the wild white-rose; the seeds are round, and blackish, about the size of a large pea.

As tea is a most important article of commerce to the Chinese, they bestow the greatest possible care upon its cultivation.

The people of China and Japan take as much pains to procure tea, of excellent quality, as the Europeans do to obtain good wine; they generally keep it a year before they use it.

Tea is propagated by seeds, which are put into holes about five inches deep, at regular distances from each other; from six to twelve being sown together, as it is supposed that only a small number grow.

When the tree is three years old, the leaves are fit to be gathered; and the men who collect them wear gloves that the flavour may not be injured. They do not pull them by handfuls, but pick them off one by one, taking great care not to break the leaves, and although this appears to be a very tedious process, each person gathers from ten to fifteen pounds a day. The tea leaves are collected at three different seasons: what are first procured, while the leaves are very young, are called imperial tea, being generally reserved for the court and people of rank, because they are considered as of the finest quality. The last gathering, when the leaves have attained their full growth, is the coarsest tea of all, and is used by the common people.

The leaves are first exposed to the steam of boiling water, after which they are put on *plates of copper*, and held over a fire until they become dry and shriveled; they are then taken off the plates with a shovel, and spread upon mats, some of the labourers taking a small quantity at a time in their hands, which they roll in one direction, while others are continually employed in stirring those on the mats, in order that they may cool the sooner, and retain their shriveled appearance. The adulteration of tea[38] has been practised in this country to an enormous extent.

[38] Adulteration of Food and Culinary Poisons, and Methods of Detecting them.—*See article Tea.*—1821.

OBSERVATIONS ON THE ART OF MAKING TEA, AND SINGULAR EFFECTS OF DIFFERENT KINDS OF TEA POTS, ON THE INFUSION OF TEA.

It has been long observed, that the infusion of tea, made in silver or polished metal tea-pots, is stronger than that which is produced in black, or other kinds of earthenware pots. This remark is explained on the principles, that polished surfaces retain heat much better than dark rough surfaces, and that, consequently, the caloric being confined in the former case, must act more powerfully than in the latter. It is further certain, that the silver or metal pot, when filled a second time, produces worse tea than the earthenware vessel; and that it is advisable to use the earthenware pot, unless a silver or metal one can be procured sufficiently large to contain, at once, all that may be required. These facts are readily explained, by considering that the action of heat, retained by the silver vessel, so far exhausts the herb, as to leave very little soluble substance for a second infusion; whereas, the reduced temperature of the water in the earthenware pot, by extracting only a small portion at first, leaves some soluble matter for the action of a subsequent infusion.

The reason for pouring boiling water into the teapot, before the infusion of the tea is made, is, that the vessel, being previously warm, may abstract less heat from the mixture, and thus admit a more powerful action. Neither is it difficult to explain the fact, why the infusion of tea is stronger if only a small quantity of boiling water be first used, and more be added some time afterwards, for if we consider that only the water immediately in contact with the herb can act upon it, and that it cools very rapidly, especially in earthenware vessels, it is clear that the effect will be greater where the heat is kept up by additions of boiling water, than where the vessel is filled at once, and the fluid suffered gradually to cool. When the infusion has once been completed, it is found that any further addition of the herb only affords a very small increase in the strength, the water having cooled much below the boiling point, and consequently acting very slightly.

JAPANESE METHOD OF MAKING TEA.

The people of Japan reduce their tea to a fine powder, which they dilute with warm water until it has acquired the consistence of a thin soup. Their manner of serving tea is as follows:—They place before the company the tea-equipage, and the caddy in which this powder is contained; they fill the cups with warm water, and taking from the caddy as much powder as the point of a knife can contain, throw it into each of the cups, and stir it, until the liquor begins to foam; it is then presented to the company, who sip it while it is warm. According to Du Halde, this method is not peculiar to the Japanese; it is also used in some of the provinces of China.

Milton Keynes UK
Ingram Content Group UK Ltd.
UKHW030617291123
433416UK00014B/824